Curtain Down at Her Majesty's

The Death of Queen Victoria in the Words of Those Who Were There

Stewart Richards

For all my children
George & Perween
Daisy, Billy & Nelly
Gordon & Alia
... wherever you are

First published 2019

The History Press
The Mill, Brimscombe Port
Stroud, Gloucestershire, GL5 2QG
www.thehistorypress.co.uk

British Library Cataloguing in Publication Data.
A catalogue record for this book is available from the British Library.

ISBN 978 0 7509 9062 2

Typesetting and origination by The History Press
Printed and bound in Great Britain by TJ International Ltd

Contents

Shortly after 6.30 p.m., the telephones and telegraph wires were suspended as Superintendent Fraser of the Household Police arranged for Osborne House to be surrounded, so as to prevent any servant or messenger from leaving.

A short while later he walked down the long gravel drive to the entrance gate, where a large crowd was waiting, and pinned a small notice on to the bulletin board:

Osborne House, Jan. 22, 6.45 p.m.

Her Majesty the Queen breathed her last at 6.30 p.m., surrounded by her children and grand-children.

JAMES REID, M.D.
R. DOUGLAS POWELL, M.D.
THOMAS BARLOW, M.D.

And so it was that the news of the Queen's passing was announced to the world.

This is the story of the last days of Queen Victoria's life and the extraordinary events surrounding her funeral, told *entirely* in the words of those who were there.

Prologue

Victoria was born on 24 May 1819, at Kensington Palace. Her father, the Duke of Kent and Strathearn, died the following year, a few days before his own father, George III.

Following the death of her uncle, William IV, in 1837, Victoria ascended the throne. She was 18 years old. Three years later she married her first cousin, Prince Albert of Saxe-Coburg and Gotha, and between 1841 and 1857 she gave birth to nine children. In 1861, after twenty years of marriage, Prince Albert, then 42, died of suspected typhoid fever.

Throughout her life, Victoria experienced further personal tragedies. In 1866, her grandson Sigismund died, followed by his brother Waldemar in 1879. In 1878, on the anniversary of the death of Prince Albert, her second daughter, Princess Alice, died of diphtheria. John Brown, her loyal servant of more than twenty years, died in 1883. Her youngest son, Prince Leopold, a haemophiliac, died in 1884 at the age of 30, after a fall while on holiday in Cannes. Her grandson, Eddy, the Duke of Clarence and Avondale, and second in line to the throne, died of influenza in 1892. And then in 1899, the 24-year-old 'Young Affie', the only son of her fourth child, Prince Alfred, Duke of Saxe-Coburg and Gotha, shot himself after an argument with his parents during their twenty-fifth wedding anniversary celebrations. In the same year, the Queen's eldest daughter Victoria, the Empress Frederick (Dowager Empress of Germany), was diagnosed with incurable breast cancer and was suffering excruciating pain. She was to die herself only a few months after her mother.

The following year, in July 1900, Victoria's son, Prince Alfred, was to die from throat cancer at the age of 55. In October, her grandson Christle died on his journey home after serving in South Africa. Then on Christmas Day, her oldest and most trusted friend, Jane, Lady Churchill, was found dead in her bed, while staying with the Queen at Osborne House.

With the Anglo-Boer War still being waged in South Africa, the 81-year-old Queen was visibly fading. Confined to a wheelchair, almost blind and suffering from severe digestive problems, she was often in pain, with lapses of memory and moments of confusion.

All these matters weighed heavily on the ageing Queen as she entered the new century.

1900

Balmoral

Cosmo Lang, Vicar of Portsea

Honorary Chaplain to the Queen and later Archbishop of Canterbury.

At Dinner I noticed that the Queen was very silent and sleepy – at times she seemed to have some difficulty in keeping awake. And after dinner she was less bright than usual and seemed to be soon tired. But though we did not think it then, there was plainly the shadow of the coming end.

John Campbell, 9th Duke of Argyll

(1845–1914) The Queen's son-in-law. Age 55. A former Liberal MP, as Marquess of Lorne he had married the Queen's fourth daughter, Princess Louise. Popular with the Queen, he was to write and publish The Life of Queen Victoria *shortly after her death in 1901.*

There had been moments of depression during the last stay at Balmoral; the weather had been cold and gray and heavy, and the Queen had not been able to enjoy her stay as usual.

Marie Mallet

As Woman of the Bedchamber, she was part of the inner circle of ladies-in-waiting who served the Queen, to whom she was devoted.

We remain in the same melancholy state here, Ladies' Dinner every night, gloomy evenings, silence only broken by the receipt of consoling telegrams in divers tongues and by the replies sent to them.

The Queen is quite angelic and does her best to keep up, but the effort is very great and cannot be good for her. The curious thing is that she said to me, '*After the Prince Consort's death I wished to die, but now I wish to live and do what I can for my country and those I love.*' Do not repeat this but it is a very remarkable utterance for a woman of eighty-two, and this is not the first time she has made the same remark. I wonder if she dreads the influence of the Prince of Wales?

When she breaks down and draws me close to her and lets me stroke her dear hand I quite forget she is far above me and only realise she is a sorrowing woman who clings to human sympathy and hungers for all that can be given on such occasions. I feel thankful for my unreserved nature and power of showing what I feel, for I believe it is a comfort to her, just a little.

I actually made the Queen laugh at dinner last night by conjuring up a vision of 'Nunks'[1] as a Bishop in full canonicals, I really thought I ought to have a medal.

She was a little brighter yesterday but still ate so little. I could kill the cooks who take no pains whatever to prepare tempting little dishes and would be a disgrace to any kitchen. How I should like to work a sweeping reform, we are abominably served just now. The footmen smell of whisky and are never prompt to

1 Alick Yorke, the Hon. Alexander Grantham Yorke, Marie's uncle and groom-in-waiting to the Queen. Described by Marie's son, Victor Mallet, as an 'elderly pansy' and the instigator of the Queen's most misquoted remark, 'We are not amused'.

answer the bell and although they do not speak rudely, they stare in such a supercilious way. As for the Queen's dinner it is more like a badly arranged picnic.

The Queen is still far from well but I hope the change to Windsor will do her good. She has so little appetite and yesterday we had a thick fog worthy of London, which made her perfectly miserable.

Windsor

John Campbell, 9th Duke of Argyll

She had felt unwell after her return to Windsor, where the very size and stateliness of the Castle appeared to oppress her, and she felt the burden of having to talk to many visitors.

The hours were at last not so punctually observed. There was increasing uncertainty as to whether the Queen would appear at lunch or dinner. She was told by the doctors that she ought to lead the life of an invalid. She must not write so much, she must do nothing to bring on unnecessary fatigue.

It was observed that her eyesight had become very dim, but she heard all that was said. Instead of holding her after-dinner talk with her guests in the corridor outside the Oak Dining-room, she was wheeled in her chair to the White Drawing-room, and sat there near the table to listen to any music played on the piano, or to call up those she desired to speak to.

Almeric Fitzroy

Chief clerk to the Privy Council. The Queen, on meeting him, remarked on how much he resembled Charles II, from whom he was descended. It also prompted Marie Mallet to comment, 'He was very much at ease, rather too much, I thought.' Considered to be indiscreet and rather gossipy.

I saw the Queen at three councils after her return to Windsor and cannot say that until the last I was struck with any marked indications of failing vitality.

So little was the Queen's mental vigour affected by the cumulative losses and anxieties of the year, that at the Council on November 12th when the transfer of seals incidental to the changes in the Cabinet took place, her memory guided us through the mazes of a somewhat intricate transaction whereon official records were dumb, and the recollections of ministers a blank.

It is true that in addition to the somewhat disquieting symptoms of loss of appetite, and an undue tendency to somnolence, periodic attacks of aphasia[2] became more frequent, and on the very day I last saw the Queen – December 10th – she was, as I afterwards learnt, unable to speak to the Brazilian ambassador, but whether it was due to the invincible optimism of courts or to a deliberate blindness, no one appears to have anticipated the impending catastrophe.

Marie Mallet

The Queen enjoyed her coffee and egg for breakfast but she still has bouts of pain and Sir James[3] is not easy. There is no reason why she should not be herself again if she could be made to take more nourishment.

The servants here are too irritating, the Queen only ordered one small dish – nouilles, for her dinner last night and it was entirely forgotten, so she had nothing. The cooks should be drawn

2 Aphasia: damage to the brain, often caused by a stroke and closely associated with dementia.

3 Sir James Reid, resident Physician in Ordinary to the Queen. He was the first physician to remain constantly at her side and to travel with her wherever she went. A shrewd, tactful and discreet courtier with a great sense of humour, he was devoted to her comfort and well-being and became one of her most trusted confidants. He was to stay with the Queen until the moment of her death.

and quartered, and the Clerks of the Kitchen strung from the Curfew Tower; their indifference makes me boil with rage.

The Queen was decidedly better this morning but a large luncheon party and shouting to the Princess of Wales[4] exhausted her and she was in pain and very feeble after it.

Of course, we must be anxious but there is no reason why she should not pick up again and regain her appetite, but she resents being treated as an invalid and as soon as she feels a tiny bit better she overtires herself and collapses. She is less meek now and that is a good sign, but Sir James has never been so anxious before in all these years.

Bernard Mallet

Husband of Marie Mallet. Private Secretary to Arthur Balfour, First Lord of the Treasury.

I had not realised that Prince Christian Victor's[5] death had been such a shock to the Queen. That and all the strain of the last year has told terribly on her.

One fears it must be the beginning of the end. But she is strong and has no disease and may probably be nursed back into comparative strength again. One prays indeed that it may be so.

Not a hint of all this appears to have reached the outside world.

---

4 Princess Alexandra, Princess of Wales, *Alix* (1844–1925). Daughter-in-law. Age 56. She was the eldest daughter of King Christian IX of Denmark. Unpretentious and kind, the Queen described her as a 'dear, lovely being'. She suffered from otosclerosis, which causes hearing loss, and was becoming increasingly deaf.

5 Prince Christian Victor of Schleswig-Holstein, *Christle* (1867–1900). Grandson. Age 33. He was the son of Princess Helena (Lenchen). Died while serving with the British Army in the Boer War under Lord Roberts.

Almeric Fitzroy

I had for some weeks been haunted with a fear that all was not right, and before the Duke of Devonshire[6] went away for Christmas I got him to go over the precedents connected with the accession ceremonies and mentioned certain points upon which I thought he should refer to the Prime Minister.[7] The first result of this move, which events quickly showed to have been anything but premature, was a protest from Lord Salisbury against '*gruesome proceedings*'; but nevertheless I obtained the Duke's permission to place myself in communication with such of the public departments the advice of which was necessary.

John Campbell, 9th Duke of Argyll

When the day fixed for the departure to Osborne arrived, those who had been told she was 'failing,' were glad to see the smile still upon her face as they took leave of her. When she entered her carriage only a few said to themselves they feared it might be the last time.

The journey to the Isle of Wight fatigued her greatly, although, as a rule, railway travelling did not affect her.

For the first time, she did not write herself the good wishes for Christmas and New Year which she was wont to send to each member of her family.

6 Spencer Compton Cavendish, 8th Duke of Devonshire. Leader of the Liberal Unionist party in the House of Lords and Lord President of the Council.

7 Robert Gascoyne-Cecil, 3rd Marquess of Salisbury. Prime Minister.

SUNDAY, 23 DECEMBER

OSBORNE HOUSE

Queen Victoria

Had a fairly good night, but again slept till nearly 12, which annoyed me very much. My appetite very indifferent. Had some broth, & later Beatrice[8] played to me on the piano. I felt rather exhausted.

Prince Arthur, Duke of Connaught and Strathearn

(1850–1942) The Queen's seventh child and reportedly her favourite son. Age 50. A committed soldier, rising to the rank of Field Marshal.

To his sister, Louise, Duchess of Argyll

Dearest Louise,[9]
Many thanks for your dear letter. I find Mama very feeble and unable to do anything she comes to no meals and goes out at odd hours, she is better today and had a good night, but I very much doubt her being able to come to the Christmas tree tomorrow – this throws quite a gloom over our already sad Xmas.

8 Beatrice, Princess Henry of Battenberg (1857–1944). Daughter. Age 43. The Queen's much-loved youngest child and constant companion. Her husband, Prince Henry of Battenberg, *Liko* (1858–96), had died four years earlier in 1896, at the age of 37, while serving with the British Army during the Anglo-Ashanti War.

9 Louise, Duchess of Argyll (1848–1939). Daughter. Age 52. A beautiful, intelligent and talented sculptor and artist. Described by her sister as '... very odd, dreadfully contradictory, very indiscreet, making mischief very frequently'. Married to John Campbell, 9th Duke of Argyll. They had no children.

You are very right in what you say about Lenchen[10] and Beatrice not reading out any of the sad accounts of poor Vicky's[11] sufferings to Mama, it is very bad for her in her present state; I will do all I can to prevent it.

There is so much that is sad just now that I feel it very difficult to make even a semblance of being cheery at Christmas time.

CHRISTMAS EVE

Queen Victoria

I got up a little earlier, & had in fact slept better, not having laid awake long. Went out with Lenchen & Beatrice. Rested when I came in. At 6 went down, being joined by Arthur, Louischen[12] & their children, Lenchen, Christian, Thora,[13] Louie,[14] & Abby,[15] & Beatrice & her children.

10 Helena, Princess Christian of Schleswig-Holstein, *Lenchen* (1846–1923). Daughter. Age 54. A lively, outspoken woman, she had married the impoverished Prince Christian of Schleswig-Holstein (1831–1917), who was fifteen years her senior. They had five children, four of whom survived infancy, including Christle who had died the previous year. With her sister Beatrice, Helena was a constant companion of the Queen.

11 Victoria, Empress Frederick of Germany, *Vicky* (1840–1901). Eldest daughter. Age 60. Her husband, Emperor Frederick III of Germany (1831–88), had died in 1888 after ruling Germany for only ninety-nine days. He was succeeded by their son, Wilhelm II. She was dying from breast cancer, which had spread to her spine and was causing her considerable pain.

12 Princess Luise, Duchess of Connaught, *Louischen* (1860–1917). Daughter-in-law. Age 40. Married to Prince Arthur, Duke of Connaught. They lived in Bagshot Park, Surrey, with their three children.

13 Princess Helena Victoria of Schleswig-Holstein, *Thora* (1870–1948). Granddaughter. Age 30. Unmarried daughter of Princess Helena, she enjoyed a very close relationship with the Queen. Her last public appearance was at the wedding of Queen Elizabeth II in 1947.

14 Princess Marie Louise of Schleswig-Holstein, *Louie* (1872–1956). Granddaughter. Age 28. Youngest daughter of Princess Helena. Her unhappy marriage to Prince Aribert of Anhalt had just been annulled.

15 Prince Albert of Schleswig-Holstein, *Abby* (1869–1931). Grandson. Age 31. Second son of Princess Helena. He joined the military, but the Prussian Army rather than the British Army and was excused service during the First World War by his cousin, the Kaiser.

We went to the Durbar Room, where the Xmas tree & present tables were arranged. I felt very melancholy as I see so very badly.

I received lovely things, amongst which an enamel of dear Christle, set with little sapphires, given by Lenchen, & a lovely bracelet, in remembrance of dear Affie,[16] given by Bertie[17] & Alix.

I gave all my personal servants their usual presents, & my children gave those for the Ladies & Gentlemen.

Took a little supper in my room, & then Beatrice came up & played to me.

Princess Beatrice

To her sister, Victoria, Empress Frederick

Dearest Vicky,
I thought so much of you on Xmas Eve, wondering how you would be spending it. I trust in not too much pain!

Dear Mama was able to come down for a short while to the Bescherung,[18] but she was very depressed and generally rather weak, her sight is so very bad and she could hardly see all her pretty presents. It was too sad how many presents were mementoes of dear departed ones.

Mama is so afraid that you may be worrying about her and about her inability to write to you, but I assured her you would not, though of course you were very sorry she was so uncomfortable and far from well.

16 Prince Alfred, Duke of Saxe-Coburg and Gotha, *Affie* (1844–1900). Son. He had died the previous summer at the age of 55.

17 Prince Albert Edward, Prince of Wales, *Bertie* (1841–1910). Eldest son. Age 59. Heir to the throne.

18 The handing out of presents: this took place on Christmas Eve in the Royal Household.

I do think she is a little better and able to take more nourishment, allowing herself to be fed every 2 hours, and she does not attempt to come to any meals, keeping quite quiet in her room, excepting when she goes out for a little,

Ever, dearest Vicky,
Your loving and attached sister,
BEATRICE.

CHRISTMAS DAY

Queen Victoria

Did not have a good night, was very restless, & every remedy that was tried failed in making me sleep. Then when I wished to get up, I fell asleep again, which was too provoking.

Went out with Lenchen & Beatrice about 1 & the former told me Sir J. Reid wished me to know that dear Jane Churchill[19] had had one of her bad heart attacks in the night, & that he had telegraphed for her son, as he thought very seriously of her condition.

Sir James Reid

To Princess Louise, Duchess of Argyll

Madam,
I felt that, as one of Lady Churchill's best friends,[20] Your Royal Highness ought to be one of the first to know.

19 Lady Jane Churchill. Age 74. A very close friend of the Queen, she was made Lady of the Bedchamber in 1854 and was the longest serving member of the Queen's Household.

20 Princess Louise had known Lady Churchill from childhood. Regardless of the difference in ages, they became close friends and were often seen together. An accomplished sculptor, Louise's first unaided bust at the age of 18 was of Lady Churchill.

I was called to her at 7.20 this morning. The Housemaid who took in her tea at 7.15 could not rouse her and called her maid, who, seeing that something serious was amiss, called me at once. I found her quite dead, having apparently been so for some time, as she was nearly cold. She looked quite placid, and I have no doubt she passed away in her sleep.

Her maid tells me she had been feeling better than usual since coming here. She was quite bright yesterday, and dined with the Royal party, who all say she was looking well and happy. Personally, it was no surprise to me: but it is most unfortunate it should have happened here and now.

The Queen does not know yet more than that she is ill and that her son has been sent for. I rather dread the effect on Her Majesty when she knows, and it is impossible to conceal it long from her.

The Queen has been eating and sleeping better the last few days and is really better again; and it is all the more sad and unfortunate that she should have this fresh shock to bear.

Queen Victoria

After I had some broth & rested a little, I took a short drive with Louischen & Thora, & we talked a great deal about dear Jane, as I was so distressed at her being so ill.

Directly I returned, I again sent for Sir James, who said '*I was just coming to tell Your Majesty all was over*.' She had died this morning early, in her sleep, & had just slept peacefully away.

They had not dared tell me for fear of giving me a shock, so had prepared me gradually for the terrible news. I saw Harriet Phipps,[21] who told me all about it. I naturally was much upset &

21 Harriet Phipps, Woman of the Bedchamber. She described their role as ladies-in-waiting to the Queen as 'We are sheets of paper on which H.M. writes with words as less trouble than using her pen and we have to convey her words as a letter would do. What you would feel free to do with a letter you are free to do with her words – no more.'

very unhappy, as dear Jane was one of my most faithful & intimate friends.

This has indeed been a terribly sad Christmas for us all!

Princess Beatrice

To her sister, Princess Louise, Duchess of Argyll

Mama now knows could [not] be kept from her any longer as she began to suspect it but through gradual preparation has so far borne the shock well though deeply affected her first thought was the grief it will be to you she wishes me to tell you this.
Beatrice.

Queen Victoria

To her daughter, Victoria, Empress Frederick

I must dictate these few lines to you as I am not well able to write myself, I have not been very well, but nothing to cause you alarm and I have not a bad pulse. I have also been able to get out a little most days.

This Christmas has been one of the saddest I ever remember, excepting '61,[22] and you are I am sure as horrified as I am at the loss of my good beloved Jane Churchill, who died in her sleep on Christmas Day. What her loss is to me I cannot describe or even realise yet, and that it should happen here is too sad, but it is I think what she would have wished, excepting for the trouble and sorrow it has caused.

22 The year Albert, Prince Consort (1819–61) died.

Almeric Fitzroy

Victor Churchill gave me some interesting details about his mother and her last intercourse with the Queen. Contrary to the usual practice, she travelled from Windsor to Osborne in the Queen's saloon, and these two, who were never again to cross the Solent alive, looked their last upon it together. It appears, for five days after her arrival at Osborne, the Queen was so prostrate that she saw no one, not even Lady Churchill. So impressed was Lady Churchill with the change, when she did see her, that she remarked to her confidential maid that the Queen was a dying woman. It fell to her lot, however, to precede her mistress by exactly four weeks. She went to her bedroom at 11.30 so well that her maid, contrary to custom, left her before she was in bed, having received orders to call her in time for early service on Christmas morning. When the hour came she had trodden the silent way. Truly, *Felix opportunitate mortis*.

MONDAY, 31 DECEMBER

Wilfrid Scawen Blunt

A poet, writer, social commentator and anti-imperialist. He was a close friend of Oscar Wilde and Winston Churchill.

The old century is very nearly out, and leaves the world in a pretty pass, and the British Empire is playing the devil in it as never an empire before on so large a scale. We may live to see its fall.

All the nations of Europe are making the same hell upon earth in China, massacring and pillaging and raping in the captured cities as outrageously as in the Middle Ages. The Emperor of Germany gives the word for slaughter and the Pope looks on and approves.

In South Africa our troops are burning farms under Kitchener's command, and the Queen and the two houses of Parliament, and the bench of bishops thank God publicly and vote money for the work.

The Americans are spending fifty millions a year on slaughtering the Filipinos; the King of the Belgians has invested his whole fortune on the Congo, where he is brutalizing the Negroes to fill his pockets. The French and Italians for the moment are playing a less prominent part in the slaughter, but their inactivity grieves them. The whole white race is revelling openly in violence, as though it had never pretended to be Christian. God's equal curse be on them all!

So ends the famous nineteenth century into which we were so proud to have been born.

I bid good-bye to the old century, may it rest in peace as it has lived in war. Of the new century I prophesy nothing except that it will see the decline of the British Empire. Other worse empires will rise perhaps in its place, but I shall not live to see the day.

And so, poor wicked nineteenth century, farewell!

Act I

Another Year Begun

1–21 January 1901

Tuesday, 1 January

The Times

The Twentieth Century begins.

Osborne House

Queen Victoria

Another year begun, I am feeling so weak & unwell, that I enter upon it sadly.

Wednesday, 2 January

Queen Victoria

Rather a better night, but slept on late into the morning, which is so provoking.

I managed to get out for ½ an hour with Lenchen & went to look at the arch which has been put in honour of Lord Roberts.[1] Drove in the afternoon with Louie[2] & Mary H,[3] getting home just in time before Lord Roberts arrived.

On Lord Roberts arrival here, I received him most warmly shaking hands with him, & he knelt down & kissed my hand.

Lord Roberts spoke with such grief of dear Christle's death & said he could not say how deeply he mourned him, & how he

---

1 Field Marshal Frederick Roberts, successful commander of the British forces in South Africa, shortly to become Commander-in-Chief, British Army.

2 Princess Marie-Louise of Schleswig-Holstein, *Louie* (1872–1956). Granddaughter. Age 28.

3 Mary Hughes, Maid of Honour.

felt for all of us.[4] It had been such a shock, as he had not had the slightest idea there was any danger, during Christle's whole illness, he had looked so well & been so cheerful.

I then gave Lord Roberts the Garter, which quite overcame him & he said it was too much. I also told him I was going to confer an Earldom on him, with the remainder to his daughter.

I felt a little tired, so rested & slept for a while.

THURSDAY, 3 JANUARY

Queen Victoria

Had a rather better night, though some broken sleep & was not up & dressed till 12. Signed some things & then went out in the garden chair.

Saw Sir A. Bigge[5] about some War Office affairs. Had not much appetite. At ½ p.3 took a short drive with Lenchen & Ismay S.[6]

FRIDAY, 4 JANUARY

Queen Victoria

Had a better night & took less draught, but still unfortunately, I slept longer than I wished.

In the afternoon drove with Harriet P. & Evelyn Moore.[7] A fine afternoon, but rather hazy. From not having been well, I see so badly, which is very tiresome.

4 Lord Roberts' son, Frederick, age 27, had died the previous year of wounds he had received at the Battle of Colenso and, like his father, he had been awarded the Victoria Cross.

5 Sir Arthur Bigge, Private Secretary to the Queen since 1895. Described by the Queen as '... a charming person, of the highest character, clever, amiable and agreeable, as well as good looking.' Rumoured to have had an affair with Princess Louise, Duchess of Argyll.

6 Ismania Fitzroy, Dowager Lady Southampton, Lady of the Bedchamber. Described by Marie Mallet as '... most kind but her dullness is beyond description.'

7 Evelyn Moore, Maid of Honour.

Had a telegram from Ld Kitchener,[8] which was satisfactory. Spent rather an uncomfortable afternoon & felt so weary & tired. Ismay S. read to me after my supper, & Beatrice came later & played to me a little on the piano.

Sir James Reid

To Marie Mallet

Dear Mrs. Mallet,
Just a line to tell you that the Queen is now much better. She has continued to improve ever since she consented to be treated as an invalid; and she now causes me no present anxiety. How far she may still improve it is impossible to say at her age: but I hope she may continue her invalid habits for some time longer, and so give herself every chance.

I have had rather an anxious time and have been very closely tied: so H.M. is to give me a little chance of air and exercise, and Sir F. Laking[9] is coming here for a week or so.

Susan[10] is in bed with a feverish chill and rheumatism but otherwise she is all right. I have been very little with her since she came, so I am longing for Sir F. Laking's arrival!

8 Lieutenant-General Herbert Kitchener, Baron Kitchener of Khartoum, Commander-in-Chief, British troops, South Africa.

9 Sir Francis Laking, personal physician to the Prince of Wales, arrived at Osborne on 5 January in order to relieve Sir James Reid, so that he could take a week's holiday. Sir James had a very low opinion of Laking's ability and considered him to be incompetent.

10 Lady Susan Reid, former Maid of Honour to the Queen. In 1899, the Queen reluctantly accepted her marriage to Sir James Reid, her resident doctor, who was eighteen years her senior. In January 1901, living at May Cottage in the grounds of Osborne, she was almost six months pregnant with their first child, having suffered an earlier miscarriage.

SATURDAY, 5 JANUARY

Queen Victoria

Had a bad & much disturbed night. Felt very exhausted. Beatrice went out with me for a short while late in the morning & in the afternoon I drove with Lenchen & Ismay S. to Newport & back. It was very fine, but cold. I was very drowsy, when I came home.

SUNDAY, 6 JANUARY

Queen Victoria

An improved night, though I wake often. Lenchen came & read letters to me after I got up. The accounts of dear Vicky are not at all satisfactory, which make me so sad.

It blew so hard & was so cold, that I did not go out in the morning. At 3 drove in a closed carriage with Lenchen & Beatrice.

Had my supper of Benger's food,[11] which is very soothing & nourishing. Saw Sir Francis Laking, who is here to relieve Sir James Reid a little.

Lady Susan Reid

To her sister-in-law, Mary Reid

Laking's visit at Osborne is a great fraud! and does not relieve Jamie of any of his work! and all our beautiful hopes of a rest and Jamie living at May Cottage [while Laking was at Osborne] have been dashed to the ground. The Queen will not see him! at least not about her health, and she can hardly bear Jamie out of her sight!

11 Benger's Food, for babies and invalids: a wheat-flour-based supplement that is made with milk to aid digestion.

She is no worse, but has ups and downs and gets very easily over tired, and when so, she gets into a nervous depressed hopeless state. However, she sleeps and eats well and Jamie says that is all one can expect just now, but her family and Miss Phipps will insist (in spite of Jamie's opinion!!) on thinking her much better than she is and it is all he can do to prevent them overtiring her, by too much talking.

The only difference Laking's visit has made is that Jamie was able to dine here twice. Last night he was to do so again but the Queen was in a nervous mood, so he gave it up, and she was so pleased and so grateful!! She does depend on him entirely now, and happily he is very well. I am quite pleased with his looks, and he is able to sleep well, now he is not disturbed at night. As things are at present Jamie thinks it is out of the question that the Queen should go abroad, and all the men of the Household are of that opinion. However, the family and Miss Phipps are still in favour of it, but I think gradually they will see for themselves that it is impossible.

Monday, 7 January

Queen Victoria

Had a much better night, but still slept on late. A very cold day with a very high wind. Took a short drive in a closed carriage, at 2.30. Dictated some letters to Lenchen.

Tuesday, 8 January

Queen Victoria

Had a restless night & woke very often. The ground was white with snow when I got up & it snowed off & on the whole morning. Got out in a closed carriage for a short while with Harriet P. I was so drowsy that I slept for 2 hours from 6 o'clock. Lenchen & Beatrice came up after their dinner.

Wednesday, 9 January

Queen Victoria

A bad night, & got up late. Did not go out till the afternoon, when I drove with Harriet P. It was fine & mild & all the snow disappearing fast.

Had some food & rested. Harriet P. read to me & later I dictated to Lenchen & then she & Beatrice wished me good night.

Thursday, 10 January

Queen Victoria

Rather a better night, but I slept on late. Only got out for a short time in the morning, & in the afternoon drove with Lenchen & Beatrice to Newport & back.

Rested when I came in, & had some food, then saw Mr Chamberlain[12] for a little while. A good telegram from Ld Kitchener.

Friday, 11 January

Queen Victoria

A better night, but felt very tired. Out in the garden chair after 1, Lenchen, Beatrice walking with me. Very fine & like spring. Went as far as Barton & back.

Felt so weary that I did not go out again in the afternoon, but slept for more than 2 hours. Afterwards Lenchen & Beatrice played duets to me, very pretty things, the 'Gondoliers', Gounod's Ballet music from 'Faust', &c. Then dictated some letters. Harriet

12 Joseph Chamberlain, industrialist, imperialist and radical politician. Leader of the Liberal Unionist party in the House of Commons, he was a principal advocate of the Second Boer War and was made Secretary of State for the Colonies in Lord Salisbury's coalition government of 1895. He was the last Cabinet minister to have an audience with the Queen.

read to me after my supper, & then Lenchen & Beatrice came up to say good night.

Saturday, 12 January

Queen Victoria

Had a good night & could take some breakfast better. There was a dense fog & no ships could cross.

Took an hour's drive at ½ p. 2 with Lenchen. It was very foggy, but the air was pleasant. Had some food when I came in & rested. Afterwards little Leopold[13] played charmingly on the violin. Took a '*lait de poule*', then signed & dictated to Lenchen. Harriet read to me after my supper & Lenchen & Beatrice came up afterwards.

Sunday, 13 January

Queen Victoria

Had a fair night, but was a little wakeful. Got up earlier & had some milk. Lenchen came & read some papers. Out before 1, in the garden chair, Lenchen & Beatrice going with me.

Rested a little, had some food, & took a short drive with Lenchen & Beatrice.

Rested when I came in & at 5.30, went down to the Drawing-room, where a short service was held, it was a great comfort to me. Rested again afterwards, then did some signing & dictated to Lenchen.

This was the Queen's final entry in the journal she had kept for more than sixty-nine years.

13 Prince Leopold of Battenberg, *Young Leopold* (1889–1922). Grandson. Age 11. The third child of Princess Beatrice, and it was through his mother that he inherited the condition haemophilia and as a result died in 1922, while undergoing a hip operation.

Monday, 14 January

Court Circular

Field-Marshal Earl Roberts, K.G., Commander-in-Chief, arrived at Osborne, and had an audience of Her Majesty before dinner.

Randall Davidson, Bishop of Winchester

A favourite of the Queen. An enormously influential cleric described by the Queen as '... singularly pleasing both in appearance and manner, very sympathetic and evidently very intelligent.' Not a view shared by all. He married Edith, daughter of Archibald Tait, the former Archbishop of Canterbury – a position he was to fill himself in 1903.

When she saw Lord Roberts the Princesses told her she must not have too long & fatiguing a talk & that they send & interrupt by a message after twenty minutes.

She answered '*Do nothing of the kind. I have a great deal to say to him which I must say & a great deal to hear from him. I shall want plenty of time.*' And she did have quite a long interview & was not a bit sleepy or confused.

Baron Eckardstein

A German diplomat serving as the German First Secretary in their London embassy. In 1898, he married Grace, the wealthy heiress of Sir John Maple of Maple's Furniture, an establishment much admired by the Queen.

While I was on a few days holiday at Cowes, rumours were current as to the serious illness of the old Queen who, as usual, had been spending Christmas at Osborne. I accordingly called there one day to enquire; and although her physician, Sir James Reid, told me her illness was by no means alarming, I learnt from various Court officials that her condition was extremely serious.

Tuesday, 15 January

Court Circular

Earl Roberts left Osborne this morning.

The Queen drove out accompanied by Her Imperial and Royal Highness the Duchess of Saxe-Coburg and Gotha.[14]

Randall Davidson, Bishop of Winchester

She did feel a few days ago that she was losing grip and that she got sleepy when talking and forgot things & said '*They will want me to give in & to have a Regency to do my work. But they are wrong. I won't. For I know they would be doing things in my name without telling me.*'

On Tuesday, though she drove out, she did get confused & since then she has attended to no business though she has had nothing of a regular 'stroke' sort, so far as I understand.

Wednesday, 16 January

Sir James Reid

The Queen had rather a disturbed night, but was very drowsy all forenoon, and disinclined to get up, although she kept saying in a semi-confused way that she must get up.

14 Princess Maria, Duchess of Saxe-Coburg and Gotha (1853–1920). Daughter-in-law. Age 47. Widow of Prince Alfred. Her father had been Emperor Alexander II of Russia.

I saw her asleep in bed in the forenoon, as I was rather anxious about her, and the maids said she was too drowsy to notice me. This was the first time I had ever seen the Queen when she was in bed. She was lying on her right side huddled up and I was struck by how small she appeared. She looked well and her breathing was quiet and normal. She did not get up till 6 p.m. when she had a dress loosely fastened round her and was wheeled into the sitting room.

At 7.30 I saw her and found her complexion good, but she was dazed, confused, and aphasic. I asked her to see Laking, as he was going away next day, and she said yes, and I got the maids to remind her.

Accordingly, at 8 he was sent for, I having told him about the Q's dazed condition. And at 8.45 as I was going down to dinner I met him coming back, and to my surprise he told me the Queen was all right, that she had been speaking to him for ¾ hour on a great many topics and was quite herself, in fact that he did not believe she was as bad as I thought. I told him it was only an instance of how wonderfully she could pull herself together when she saw anyone but her maids or me, and that I should not wonder if she were quite confused again after he had left. 10 minutes later I was sent for by the maids and found H.M. quite exhausted and as confused as ever. She went back to bed at once.

I wrote tonight to the Prince of Wales and told him exactly what I thought about the Queen. I felt now so anxious about the Queen that I told Miss Phipps I should so much like to get Sir D. Powell[15] to come and see H.M. with me, the difficulty being how to tell the Queen without frightening her. I had already written privately to Powell this morning telling him I was very anxious and might want him on short notice, and that he was to be ready to come at once.

---

15 Sir Richard Douglas Powell, Physician in Ordinary to the Queen and a highly regarded friend and colleague of Sir James Reid.

Sir Frederick Ponsonby

Known as Fritz, he was a witty, resourceful and punctilious courtier with impeccable manners and a domineering personality. Following in the footsteps of his father, Sir Henry Ponsonby, who had been Private Secretary to the Queen until his death in 1895, Fritz became assistant Private Secretary to Sir Arthur Bigge, who had replaced his father as the Queen's Private Secretary.

In 1900 the Queen made a new arrangement which necessitated my sleeping at Osborne House instead of Barton Manor. The increasing number of telegrams in addition to occasional telephone messages that were often received at night made it necessary for someone who could deal with them to sleep at Osborne House. The Queen therefore decided that I was to sleep at Osborne House in future and deal with any emergency that might arise.

Once in February 1900, the Queen's health not being good, Sir James Reid asked me to take steps to ensure that no bad news should reach her by telegram. I had not found this quite so easy to arrange as I anticipated, for when I told Mr. Hiley, the telegraph clerk, to bring me any telegram that might come for the Queen before sending it in to her, he replied he had strict orders from her that all telegrams addressed to her were to be sent in at once to her and to no one else. I had spoken in a careless manner so that there should be no suspicion that anything was wrong, but I grasped that I should have to take him into my confidence. I therefore told him the Queen was unwell and that Sir James Reid had impressed on me the necessity of her not being worried by bad news, and I finally wrote down and signed instructions to him enjoining secrecy.

When, therefore, Reid came to me on January 16, 1901, and told me the Queen was not well, I did not think it serious, but repeated the former instructions to the telegraph clerk.

THURSDAY, 17 JANUARY

Sir James Reid

The Queen had a quiet night, but in the morning, was, when I saw her in bed, very confused, aphasic and drowsy. I did not at all like her condition, and thought she might be getting comatose, and might in fact die within a few days.

I at once saw Princess Beatrice and Princess Christian [Helena], and told them I was very anxious and that I wanted Powell at once, to which they consented, and I wired asking him to come by the first train he could catch. When I told Laking what I had done, he said he would like to stay another day to 'help' me.

Lady Susan Reid

Laking is no good. Last night he saw the Queen and thought her wonderfully well!!! and Jamie saw her after he did and thought her all wrong. By what Jamie said this morning (though I saw him so hurriedly) I fear there is not much hope. It is wonderful what he has been to her all these years, and now, if the end comes, I know it will be a wrench to him, and what a sensation in the world! The only consolation is that I don't think one could wish her to live in a state of childishness, which from the present state of her brain seems inevitable.

Princess Christian (Helena)

To the Marquess of Salisbury

January 17, 1901 1.30pm
Today The Queen has developed some difficulty of speech, mental confusion and drowsiness which Sir James Reid does not

like and makes him very uneasy. We have sent for Sir D. Powell. Will keep you informed.

Sir James Reid

The Queen was fairly quiet all the afternoon but staid [sic] in bed till 7 p.m. when she got out of bed, and was wheeled to her sitting room, dressed as last night. She asked the Princesses if people were beginning to be frightened about her, as she had not been out for 2 days, and when Princess Christian [Helena] said the weather had been so bad that people would not be surprised, she replied that the people knew she always went out in rain!

In the evening I was rung up specially on the telephone by Mrs Tuck,[16] who said the Q wanted to know how I was, as she was afraid I would break down and be ill, and that I must have help, and I must not be allowed to break down, as *'he is the only one that understands me'*.

Being so anxious to prepare the public for what I feared was coming, and also thinking that her condition was too serious for it to be kept longer from the public, I thought a statement ought to be made in the Court Circular, and accordingly Bigge and I drew up a paragraph which we wished to be put in tomorrow's circular, and in it we mentioned that I had sent for Sir D. Powell. Before sending it off, Bigge telephoned it to Marlboro' House for the P. of W.'s approval, but got a reply saying H.R.H. wished no statement whatever to be made, so we were obliged to cancel it.

Powell arrived at 7.30, and I told the Queen that he was in the island and had called to see me, and, as he was in the house, I hoped she would see him. She expressed no surprise (as she would have done in her usual condition) and said certainly. So

16 Mary Tuck, principal dresser to the Queen since 1892. Living in close proximity with the Queen, she was on constant duty, and she would have borne the burden of Victoria's increasing insomnia, as Sir James noted: 'Every time she wakes, even for a few minutes, she rings for her maids, who of course don't like it, and naturally call the night a "bad" one.'

at 8.15 he saw H.M. with me for a few minutes. She was rather apathetic and did not pull herself together at all (for the first time) on seeing a stranger. She said nothing to him, except to answer rather incoherently the few questions he put to her.

On leaving the room Powell said to me there could be no possible doubt as to her having cerebral degeneration, and that her condition was precarious but not hopeless.

CHATSWORTH HOUSE, DERBYSHIRE

Margot Asquith

The lively but unconventional political hostess who was married to the future Liberal Prime Minister, Herbert Henry Asquith.

My husband and I were staying at Chatsworth. There was a huge house party, including Arthur Balfour[17] and [Joseph] Chamberlain. Before going down to dinner, Henry came into my bedroom and told me he had had a telegram to say that Queen Victoria was very ill and he feared the worst; he added that it was a profound secret and that I was to tell no one.

After dinner I was asked by the Duchess'[18] granddaughters, Lady Aldra and Lady Mary Acheson to join them at planchette,[19] so, to please them, I put my hand upon the board. I was listening to what the Duchess was saying and my mind was a blank. After the girls and I had scratched about for a little time, one of them took the paper off the board and read out loud: '*The Queen is*

---

17 Arthur Balfour, Conservative MP, First Lord of the Treasury, Leader of the House of Commons. He was also nephew of the Prime Minister, Lord Salisbury, who he was to succeed as Prime Minister in 1902, leading to the saying 'Bob's your uncle'.

18 Louisa Cavendish, Duchess of Devonshire, known as the 'double duchess', having previously married William Montagu, 7th Duke of Manchester.

19 Planchette: an early form of Ouija.

dying.' She added, '*What Queen can that be?*' We gathered round her and all looked at the writing; and there I read distinctly out of a lot of hieroglyphics: '*The Queen is dying.*'

If the three of us had combined to try to write this, and had poked about all night, we could not have done it.

To the Editor of The Times

Sir,
To-morrow (18th) our gracious Queen, who was born May 24, 1819, will have lived 81 years 239 days, exactly the age of her grandfather, King George III., when he died on January 29, 1820, he having been born on June 4, 1733 (new style); so after tomorrow his granddaughter will take his place as living the longest life as well as reigning the longest reign.
Canterbury, Jan.17.
CYRIL A. GREAVES

Friday, 18 January

London

Court Circular

The Queen has not lately been in her usual health, and is unable for the present to take her customary drives. The Queen during the past year has had a great strain upon her powers, which has rather told upon Her Majesty's nervous system. It has therefore been thought advisable by Her Majesty's physicians that the Queen should be kept perfectly quiet in the house, and should abstain for the present from transacting business.

Arthur Bigge

To Lord Salisbury

Jan 18, 1901
The doctors say it will be impossible for the Queen to sign warrants or transact any business for the present.

Please let me know what you wish to be done regarding the current work of which there is naturally some accumulation.

A.G.C. Liddell

Assistant secretary in the Lord Chancellor's department.

The Lord Chancellor came in after the cabinet & said that the Queen had had a paralytic stroke & it was a question of what should be done [as] to her signature.

I told him that I had read that George IV used a stamp during his last illness. On looking into the matter we found an autograph signature of George IV on a bill of January 1830 – 9th May of same year we discovered a Royal Assent to an Act of Parliament signed by a stamped signature of the Kings (attested by the Duke of Wellington and Lord Farnborough).

I have one of the last documents signed with this stamp & attested by The Duke of Wellington & Lord Farnham, it bears the date of 25 June 1830, the King died 26 June. It authorises the payment of the expenses incurred on account of the funeral of our late dearly beloved Brother the Duke of York. The amount is £3136 12/-

Lady Violet Cecil

Married to Lord Edward Cecil, fourth son of the Prime Minister, Lord Salisbury.

Soon there was news which was to overshadow all else. The Queen was ill. She had had a stroke. It was doubtful whether she would ever do business again. Lord Salisbury was very unhappy. He was devoted to the Queen; the break for him would be tremendous. The Queen had had, in spite of her great courage, a fearful year. She felt the public disasters tremendously, and the Empress Frederick's illness, Prince Christian Victor's death, the sudden death of her old friend, Lady Churchill, had all piled up on her. And over all the war. She was the first person one thought of when the military disasters and losses were occurring.

Sir Edward Hamilton

Civil servant in the Treasury and political diarist.

The Queen is unwell – presumably her indisposition is serious for two of Her Doctors went down last night. They will make as light of the illness as they can – Royalties always pooh-pooh illness.

Today She has lived exactly as long as George III. So, She will be the longest-lived sovereign we have ever had as well as the longest-reigning one.

Is it the beginning of the end? One trusts that at any rate there will be no lingering; and that physical strength will not out-last mental strength. We have come to regard the Queen so much in the light of a permanent institution that it is almost impossible to imagine Her passing away or to form any idea of the effect it would have throughout the world.

OSBORNE HOUSE

Princess Helena

To the Prince of Wales

January 18, 1901 10.45 am
Queen continues in the same condition. She is no worse and there are no fresh unfavourable symptoms. Will report again later in the day and also this evening. Sir F Laking returns today and will report details to you personally.
Helena

Sir James Reid

Queen had a fair night; little change from yesterday. She remained in bed all day until 8 p.m. and I saw her at frequent intervals. She took food well, mostly in liquid form. Her mind was fairly clear but there was some aphasia and the articulation was bad. The right side of her face was rather flat, and the left side drooping. She slept much and was very weak.

Laking left for London at 1 o'clock to my great relief, as he took up so much of my time by talking and was no help to me.

Knowing that the Kaiser[20] relied on me to let him know if his grandmother was very ill, I sent him this telegram: '*Disquieting symptoms have developed which cause considerable anxiety. This is private. Reid*.' No one knew I had sent it, as I knew the Princesses would disapprove.

In the afternoon she said to me, '*Is there anyone in the house?*' I did not know what she meant, but she at once added, '*Is the Prince*

20 Wilhelm II, Emperor of Germany and King of Prussia (1859–1941). Eldest grandson. Age 41. Reid had grown to like the Kaiser during his many visits to the Isle of Wight and had promised to keep him informed of his 'Grandmamma's health'.

of Wales here? I said no, but that he could come if she would like to see him, and she replied '*I do not advise it at present.*'

Sir Arthur Bigge

To Sir Francis Knollys[21]

18 January 1901
Both Reid & Powell think it would be advisable for the Prince not to leave London for the present but Sir Laking who reached London about 6 will be able to give all particulars that would enable HRH to decide for himself.

Sir James Reid

In the evening I got, to my great surprise, a telegram from Laking who had just seen the Prince of Wales, saying, '*Everything considered quite satisfactory. He hopes to go to the country until Monday*', meaning Sandringham where he was to receive guests, Laking evidently not yet realising the gravity of the situation, or at all events not having impressed the Prince with it.

George, Duke of York

(1865–1936) Grandson. Age 35. Second son of the Prince of Wales, he was second in line to the throne after the sudden death of his elder brother, Albert Victor (Eddy), Duke of Clarence and Avondale (1864–92), from influenza during the pandemic in January 1892. Later to become King George V.

21 Sir Francis Knollys, Private Secretary to the Prince of Wales. An appointment strongly opposed by the Queen who did not think him clever enough. Popular with the rest of the Royal Family, who called him 'Fooks'. At the time of the Queen's death he was described as '... the most powerful man in England at this moment'.

When we got to the Club, Papa told me that darling Grandmama had had a slight stroke this morning. He got a cypher telegram tonight from Aunt Helena saying her condition was precarious but no immediate danger. It makes us all very anxious. Grandmama has not been well for some weeks now.

Sir James Reid

Bigge telephoned to Marlborough House that he was overwhelmed with telegraphic and other enquiries regarding the Queen's health about which alarming reports were already in circulation, and that he thought some statement must be published; and the Prince of Wales then consented to the publication tomorrow of a modification by him of the statement we had wished to publish this morning, omitting the most alarming part of it as well as the fact that Powell had been summoned to Osborne.

SATURDAY, 19 JANUARY

LONDON

The Times

Rare indeed have been the occasions throughout her long reign when her Majesty has failed to transact the daily business which presses so heavily and inevitably upon the wearer of the imperial crown of Great Britain. We note that it is only since Tuesday that she has inter-mitted her drives, and that on Monday she gave an audience to Lord Roberts. We trust that her physicians have insisted betimes on perfect quiet, and we must find consolation in the words 'for the present' in their communication about the transaction of business.

Daily News

As all her Majesty's subjects know, her love of fresh air has taken her out of doors in the most inclement weather. It cannot be doubted that the health of her Majesty is precarious.

Daily Express

Perhaps the best evidence that the grave anxiety which was aroused by the reports of her Majesty's health yesterday is groundless, lies in the fact that the Duke of York left London for Sandringham yesterday afternoon and that the Prince of Wales will follow him thither today, leaving St Pancras by the 2.35 train.

Osborne House

Sir James Reid

The Queen passed a fair night, but was rather worse in the morning, being very weak, wandering, and incoherent, taking food well but in an automatic way; tongue furred.

Princess Christian [Helena], who was sending daily telegraphic reports to the Prince of Wales, still took a sanguine view and wrote a favourable report this morning, saying '*the Queen had passed a good night, was taking food well, and that she felt happier about her*', but ignoring all the essential and unfavourable points.

In the meantime I happened to go to Bigge's room just as he was in telephonic communication with Sir Francis Knollys at Marlborough House, who was asking him for the Prince of Wales how the Queen was, and whether he should go to Sandringham as arranged. Seeing me come in, Bigge asked Knollys to wait a minute, as I had just come in and he would get my opinion, which I gave as follows: '*Tell the Prince of Wales that in my opinion he ought not to go to Sandringham but to remain in London ready to come here at a moment's notice; that I consider the Queen's condition is a most serious one, and that I think it quite possible she might be dead within a few days.'* After this had been done, Princess Christian's [Helena] message was sent by her for Bigge to cypher, and Bigge, struck by its tenor so contradictory to mine, went up to see the Princess and point this out to her before sending it.

She sent for me at once, while Bigge was there, and rather angrily upbraided me for sending such a report in contradiction to hers. (She did not want the Prince to come, and for some days had been telling me how undesirable it would be for the Prince and Princess of Wales to come). I replied that I had told the Prince of Wales my exact opinion, that I considered the Queen was worse, and in a very dangerous state, whereas anyone getting her telegrams would naturally conclude that H.M. was going on satisfactorily and form an opinion of her progress the reverse of the truth: but that when I was asked my opinion I gave it.

She was much annoyed at first, but she soon calmed down, and said, '*Then the Prince had better come*'.

Princess Helena

To the Prince of Wales

We beg you to come here as we so terribly anxious.
Helena

Sir James Reid

Powell saw the Queen with me repeatedly during the day, and we issued our first bulletin in the forenoon.

Bulletin – Osborne, 19 January, noon

The Queen is suffering from great physical prostration accompanied by symptoms that cause anxiety.
R. DOUGLAS POWELL, M.D.
JAMES REID, M.D.

Sir James Reid

Before luncheon I met the Princesses Christian [Helena] and Beatrice who had just heard that the Kaiser was starting today for England with the Duke of Connaught (who was in Germany for the Anniversary of something[22] and had been telegraphed for to return). They were most excited about it and said the Kaiser must be stopped at all hazards, and that they had telegraphed to the Duke of Connaught to do so.

This rather startled me as I had no doubt the Kaiser was coming on account of my secret telegram to him, which they knew nothing about, and I thought I might get into a pretty row if it came out I had sent it.

Berlin

Wilhelm II, Emperor of Germany

To the British Ambassador, Berlin

I have duly informed the Prince of Wales, begging him that no notice whatever is taken of me as Emperor and that I come as

22 The Duke of Connaught was in Berlin, attending the celebrations marking the 200th anniversary of the establishment of the Prussian monarchy.

grandson. I suppose the 'petticoats' who are fencing off poor grandmamma from the world – and I fear, often from me – will kick up a row when they hear of my coming; but I don't care for what I do is my duty, the more so as it is this 'unparalleled' grandmamma, as none ever existed before. I leave with Uncle Arthur.[23] Am sorry, very sorry.

Osborne House

Sir James Reid

I had still more misgivings, as the Queen in the afternoon and evening became clearer in intellect, and I feared that this being so, the agitation of the Kaiser's coming, if she realised it, might give her the impression that we considered her dying, and help to turn the scale in the wrong direction.

I thought of telegraphing to Flushing to stop the Kaiser, or, at all events, to warn him that if he came he could not see his grandmother at present, but Bigge informed me that the Government had already sent a ship to meet and escort him: so I gave up the idea.

London

Reginald Brett, Viscount Esher

Permanent Secretary to the Office of Works, he was responsible for the high-profile success of the Queen's diamond jubilee in 1897. Although happily married with four children, he continued to have relationships with other men; most notoriously he had a passionate

23 Arthur, Duke of Connaught.

relationship with his youngest son, Maurice, while his son was still at Eton.

To his son, Maurice[24]

Bigge telegraphed that I am not to go to Osborne on Monday owing to the Queen's illness. It does not surprise me. There was no Court Circular for Thursday and the rumours were very persistent. T. went to Kensington Palace, and saw Princess Louise, who was starting for Osborne with the Prince of Wales. It is, I fear, the end. What a change!

Court Circular

The Prince of Wales, left Victoria Station by special train for Portsmouth en route to Osborne to visit the Queen. The train was timed for departure at 1 30, but it was kept waiting for Princess Louise (Duchess of Argyll), who arrived at 1 50, and left in company with the Prince to visit her Majesty.

Osborne House

Sir Arthur Bigge

To the Bishop of Winchester[25]

19 January 1901
Condition very serious Family summoned.
Bigge

---

24 Maurice Vyner Baliol Brett, younger son of Reginald Brett, Viscount Esher. Served with distinction during the Great War rising to the rank of lieutenant-colonel. He edited his father's letters and journals for publication.

25 Randall Davidson.

The Times

The Prince of Wales and Princess Louise arrived at Portsmouth at 4 o'clock, and as the viaduct connecting the Harbour Station is still under repair, owing to its having been run into by an Isle of Wight packet some months ago, their Royal Highnesses had to drive into the dockyard. The Majestic, flagship of the Channel Squadron, which was lying end on to the Alberta, furnished a guard of honour, but the Prince of Wales, who did not wait to inspect the guard, hurried on board the Royal yacht, and left at once for Osborne. As the visit to the Queen was of a strictly private and family character no salutes were fired.

Sir James Reid

The Prince arrived at 5 p.m., the Princess of Wales coming from Sandringham late in the evening.

About 6 o'clock, when I was seeing the Queen, she was clear and talked to me coherently though with difficulty. Among other things she said to me, '*Am I better? I have been very ill*' I said, '*Yes, Y.M. has been very ill but you are now better.*' She added, '*You must be very tired, but you must not break down, you ought to have help*.' I told her Sir Richard [Douglas Powell] was with me and was a great help, which seemed to please her. Then she said, '*There is much better news from South Africa today*', evidently referring to some telegram which the Princesses had mentioned to her, and showing how even then she had got the war in her mind. She next said, '*I think the Prince of Wales should be told I have been very ill, as I am sure he would feel it.*' I replied '*H.R.H. does know as I have reported to him all that I think Y.M. would wish me to tell him, and Sir F. Laking who went back yesterday has also told him. He is most concerned and is anxious to come as soon as Your Majesty would like to see him. Would Y.M. like him to come now?*' She replied '*Certainly, but he needn't stay.*'

(The Prince was already in the house.) All this made me think the Queen was really better, and I again became hopeful that she might still pull through after all, though of course still most anxious and feeling that a day or two would decide one way or the other.

Later on when I went to see her with Powell, she said to Mrs Tuck, '*I want everybody to go out except Sir James*', and so they all went out leaving me alone with her.

When I told her that everybody had gone out, she looked in my face and said, '*I should like to live a little longer, as I have still a few things to settle. I have arranged most things, but there are still some left, and I want to live a little longer.*' She appealed to me in this pathetic way with great trust as if she thought I could make her live.

In the evening we issued a rather more favourable bulletin.

Bulletin – Osborne, 19 January, 6 p.m.

The Queen's strength has been fairly maintained
throughout the day, and there are indications
of slight improvements in the symptoms
this evening.
JAMES REID, M.D.
R. DOUGLAS POWELL, M.D.

I had several interviews with the Prince of Wales who was very nice, and quite agreed that it was better the Queen should not know he was in the house.

I gathered however from the Princesses that, as H.M. was rather better, the Prince of Wales thought he had been brought down rather on false pretences and to some extent '*made a fool of'* as they put it. He did not however say this to me, but only that my message in the morning had greatly surprised him. I asked him to see Powell with me, that he might hear that he took an equally serious view with me, which he did.

The Prince of Wales took up the view of the Princesses as to the inadvisability of the Kaiser's visit, and said the only thing he could now do was to go up to London tomorrow to meet him and keep him at Buckingham Palace, on the grounds that he could not be allowed to see the Queen at present, and this also made the Prince of Wales decline my offer to let him see the Queen from the door of her bedroom (without her knowledge), as he said he wished to be able to give the Kaiser his word of honour that not even he (the Prince of Wales) had been allowed to see her.

Lady Susan Reid

Jamie is privately astonished at Princess Beatrice not being more concerned and upset about her Mother's condition. She takes it all very calmly, and was out yesterday when the Queen sent to say she would see her!! I think Princess Christian [Helena] has more feeling. She has shut her eyes wilfully to the truth for so long, that now it is a shock.

Sir James Reid

Louise [Duchess of Argyll] is as usual, much down on her sisters. Hope she won't stay long, or she will do mischief!

Lord Edward Pelham-Clinton

Master of the Household since 1894, he was in charge of all domestic staff and housekeeping arrangements.

Rain nearly all day and a S.E. gale. At home all day. Busy. Lady Monson, Fraulein Gazerl and Miss Moore leave to make room in the house for Royal Family coming. Royal dinner of six. Household dinner fourteen.

Queen rather better at six o'clock bulletin.

London

The Times

The Princess of Wales, attended by Miss Knollys,[26] arrived at Marlborough House at 6 20, having travelled by special train from Sandringham. The Princess of Wales made but a brief stay at Marlborough House. Driving to Victoria, her Royal Highness, left by special train for Portsmouth at 6 50.

When the Princess left Sandringham the Duke of York was out shooting, and his Royal Highness did not receive the grave news about her Majesty until later. This explains why his Royal Highness did not accompany the Princess.

Randall Davidson, Bishop of Winchester

I was sitting with Mrs. Creighton[27] at Fulham [Palace] when a telegram reached me. It was from Sir Arthur Bigge, stating that the Queen's condition had become most serious and that the family had been summoned.

I was engaged to preach next day at Holloway College, and was going thither from Fulham, but I decided to go at once to Osborne, though Bigge had not exactly summoned me to do so.

26 Charlotte Knollys, Lady of the Bedchamber to the Princess of Wales; her brother Sir Francis Knollys was Private Secretary to the Prince of Wales.

27 Louise Creighton, widow of the Bishop of London, Mandell Creighton, who had died a few days earlier.

I got back to Waterloo and telegraphed to Holloway College, stating that I could not come; to the Dean of Windsor, asking him to provide for my place there; to Sir Arthur Bigge, stating that I would come to Cowes that night and sleep there unless he summoned me to his house at Osborne.

Fortunately, on Saturday night there is a late boat from Southampton to Cowes. The journey was most unpleasant, as it was a stormy night with some rain, and the train does not on those occasions run from the Dock Station to the Pier. We were packed into some cabs provided by the Railway Company. My companions were Press men and telegraph clerks, and on the boat we found a great company of footballers, rather boisterous. Altogether it was a strange companionship in an hour of such anxiety.

On reaching Cowes about 11 p.m. I found a letter from Bigge stating that every room in the Osborne houses was full and that the immediate anxiety was relieved. Launcelot Smith[28] met me and I went to his Vicarage.

Sir James Reid

Was up all night and fetched Powell repeatedly, as she was very confused and restless and evidently worse. We, for the first time, began giving her oxygen during the night.

28 Rev. Launcelot Smith, Vicar of St Mary's.

Sunday, 20 January

London

Daily Chronicle

The hush of an invisible presence is over the land. Queen Victoria lies at Osborne in a critical condition, surrounded by her family and consoled by the love of her innumerable subjects.

Lord Gower

Liberal MP and sculptor. The youngest son of the Duke of Sutherland and generally accepted as being the model for Oscar Wilde's Lord Henry Wotton in The Picture of Dorian Gray. *His nephew was John Campbell, 9th Duke of Argyll.*

Very alarming reports of the Queen's health have appeared in the papers during the last two days; we hear that the Prince of Wales and Princess Louise have gone to Osborne. In a letter I received from Argyll a few days ago, he said they were to go to Osborne to-morrow, the 21st. I much fear it is the beginning of the end. One cannot realise what a loss her death would be to everyone.

Reginald Brett, Viscount Esher

The Kaiser and the Duke of Connaught are coming straight from Berlin. The news from Osborne is as sad as it can be. But what a comfort that the end of this long and splendid reign should come so rapidly. No lingering illness. The Queen drove out on Tuesday. To-day she is at the point of death.

Bulletin – Osborne, 20 January, 11 a.m.

The Queen has passed a somewhat restless night.
There is no material change in her condition since
the last report.
R. DOUGLAS POWELL, M.D.
JAMES REID, M.D.

BERLIN

The Times

Berlin. The German Emperor, on receiving yesterday morning grave news regarding the condition of the Queen, determined to proceed at once to England. But as the Flushing express had left it was arranged by the Emperor that his Royal uncle should accompany him in his Majesty's special train. The Imperial train had been kept in readiness with steam up at the Potsdamer Station during the greater part of the day. At 11 a.m. his Majesty paid a visit of half-an-hour's duration to the British Ambassador, Sir Frank Lascelles, who throughout the day had been in frequent conference with the Duke of Connaught at the Royal Castle and at the Embassy.

As 6 o'clock approached the Emperor and the Duke of Connaught drove rapidly together in a closed Court carriage to the Potsdamer Railway Station, whence the Imperial train started for Flushing at 6 o'clock.

When it became known that the Emperor was about to proceed to England arrangements were immediately made by the British Admiralty for the despatch of the cruiser Minerva to meet his Majesty at Flushing. But when it became evident that the Minerva could hardly arrive at the Dutch port in time one of the Royal Mail Zeeland steamers was chartered and the Emperor and the Duke of Connaught, who arrived at Flushing this morning, embarked upon that vessel for England.

Court Circular

His Royal Highness the Prince of Wales, left Osborne this morning for London to meet His Imperial Majesty the German Emperor.

Baron Holstein

Fritz von Holstein, head of the political department at the German Foreign Office.

To Baron Eckardstein

I hope urgently that the Royal Family will not get on the wrong side of the Kaiser with their usual lack of consideration. Do your best with the British Ministers, or anyhow see that something is at once done to make them insist on courteous treatment for the Kaiser. The Chancellor has just said to me that he thought the news very ominous that the Kaiser had not been allowed to come to Osborne. I suggest that if our representations to the British Ministers produce good results you should let His Majesty know it in some way that will not be directly derogatory to his relatives.
HOLSTEIN

LONDON

Baron Eckardstein

[The Kaiser] arrived with his suite on the Dutch mail-boat at Port Victoria, where I met him with the Embassy staff.

When I met the Kaiser on board he thanked me for enabling him to arrive in time at the sick-bed of his grandmother. He said he would go on the very next morning to Osborne, and hoped to God he would still find the Queen alive. He had been bombarded all through his journey with telegrams from his aunts at Osborne telling him to go back. But he would not take the risk of doing this as he should never have forgiven himself while he lived, if the end had come and he had not arrived in time.

He took me with him in his saloon-carriage to London as he wished to learn from me what had been happening. I reported to him fully my conversations with the Duke of Devonshire and Chamberlain at Chatsworth, and he expressed himself as highly delighted with the pronouncement of the two Ministers as to an Anglo-German alliance.

The Times

Shortly before 4 o'clock, a large crowd assembled at Victoria Station in consequence of the news that the Prince of Wales was expected back in town to meet the German Emperor. He [the Prince of Wales] arrived by special train at 3 47. The Court officials inquired anxiously about the Queen, and they gathered from the fact that his Royal Highness had been enabled to leave Osborne that the state of affairs was on the whole more favourable, for the Prince replied, '*You see they have let me come away*.'

There was much eagerness on the part of the public to see the German Emperor on his arrival in London. The chief point of attraction was Charing-cross terminus, where the sanding of carriage ways, the regulation of traffic, and the laying of scarlet cloth on the platform had been early taken in hand.

As the dimensions of the crowd grew the officials were reluctantly compelled to put up barriers and to post constables, so as to exclude the general body of spectators from the station. Just before the arrival of the special train was expected, the Prince of Wales drove into the enclosure.

The special train arrived at the platform at 6 20. The Emperor and the Duke of Connaught were seen standing in their saloon ready to leave the train. The Emperor, who looked well but appeared to be anxious, was in ordinary civilian dress. The Prince of Wales stepped into the saloon and greeted his kinsman. They drove away to Buckingham Palace, and as the carriage passed between the lines of people in the streets almost complete silence was observed.

Wilhelm II, Emperor of Germany

I was cordially received in London by the Prince of Wales and the royal family. As my carriage drove at a trot from the railway station, a plainly dressed man stepped forward from the closely packed crowd standing there in absolute silence, to the side of the carriage, bared his head, and said: '*Thank you, Kaiser!*' The Prince of Wales added: '*That is what they all think and they will never forget this visit of yours.*' Nevertheless, they did forget it, and quickly.

OSBORNE HOUSE

Randall Davidson, Bishop of Winchester

It was the day for the commemoration of Prince Henry's death[29] in Whippingham Church, and Parratt[30] had come from Windsor for the occasion. I sent a letter from Bigge's house to Princess Beatrice, stating that I should be in Whippingham Church and take part in the Service, and was ready to be of any further use if desired. A message came back begging me to go to Osborne House immediately after the Service.

I did so and had much talk with different members of the Family. The Doctors thought the Queen was rather better and wished to keep her perfectly quiet: even her daughters were not seeing her. I accordingly arranged to sleep at Whippingham Rectory. I attended Whippingham Church at 6 o'clock and preached. There was a good congregation, evidently in anxious strain. We added some special prayers to the Service, and I tried to say something helpful.

Sir James Reid

As [the Queen] was now quite unable to do anything for herself it was most difficult for the nurse and her maids to manage her in the large double bed: so in the morning we decided to try to move her onto a smaller bed.

Woodford[31] and his two men brought a screen, which the maids and I put round her bed, so that the men could not see her while they brought in and fitted together the small bed, which was in

29 Prince Henry of Battenberg, *Liko* (1858–96). Son-in-law, late husband of Princess Beatrice, who had died on 20 January 1896.

30 Sir Walter Parratt, Master of the Queen's Musick and organist of St George's Chapel, Windsor.

31 Head of works at Osborne House.

parts. They then went out, and the maids and I removing the screen wheeled the small bed close to the Queen's, and after a good deal of difficulty we together lifted her on to it. During this operation she seemed but vaguely conscious of what we were doing, though her face at times expressed discomfort. We then wheeled the small bed on which we had moved her into the corner, and put up the screen round it, while Woodford and his two men came in again and pushed the big bed out of the way towards the fireplace. This being done they retired, and we wheeled the Queen back into the position her large bed had occupied.

This change we found a very great advantage during the next two days.

During the day she took food fairly well, but was very apathetic and aphasic, and hardly ever intelligible. Powell and I were again most anxious.

Bulletin – Osborne, 20 January, 4.30 p.m.

Her Majesty's strength has been fairly maintained throughout the day. Although no fresh developments have taken place, the symptoms continue to cause anxiety.

JAMES REID, M.D.
R. DOUGLAS POWELL, M.D.

Lord Edward Pelham-Clinton

Fine and bright rather high wind. The Anniversary of Prince Henry of Battenberg's death; a Service held at Whippingham. I do not attend it. I walk by the sea between 4 and 5. The Queen about the same at 5 o'clock – all very anxious.

Sir James Reid

In the evening the Queen was almost quite unconscious and had much difficulty in swallowing. I told all the Princesses that they might go and see the Queen now without any fear of doing harm. This they did, but she recognised none of them.

As the condition was so bad, I telegraphed to Barlow,[32] asking him to come and join Powell and me tomorrow morning by the 7.55 train, reaching Cowes at 12.10: but later on fearing this might be too late, I again telegraphed asking him to start if possible by the 5.40 a.m. train, reaching Cowes at 9.30. This I did in accordance with the Queen's private written instructions to me for the event of her serious illness.

Sir Frederick Ponsonby

After dinner a long telegram about the war in South Africa arrived and I went off to ask Reid what should be done with it. He said with a grave face that there had been a change for the worse and that he feared that the end might come at any time during the night. I therefore dispatched a mounted groom to summon Edwards[33] and Bigge and I also sent a carriage for the Bishop of Winchester.

Bulletin – Osborne, 20 January, Midnight

The Queen's condition has late this evening become more serious, with increase of weakness and diminished power of taking nourishment.
JAMES REID, M.D.
R. DOUGLAS POWELL, M.D.

32 Sir Thomas Barlow, Physician Extraordinary to the Queen.

33 Sir Fleetwood Edwards, Keeper of the Privy Purse and Extra Equerry to the Queen.

They all came and it was decided that the Prince of Wales should be told at once.

The telephone in those days for long-distance calls was very uncertain, but after some delay I managed to get on to the Prince of Wales himself; and he decided to come at once by special train.

M'Neill had retired to bed and so I had to make the arrangements about the yacht Alberta going off at once to Portsmouth to meet the Prince of Wales, but just as I was telephoning to Captain Broad I received a message that the Queen had again rallied and that there was no necessity for the Prince of Wales to come down that night. To cancel the instructions to the yacht only took a minute, but stopping the Prince of Wales was more difficult. However, eventually I got a message through to Marlborough House.

Randall Davidson, Bishop of Winchester

1.30 a.m.
My beloved wife,
I think I must write a few lines now at what is certainly one of the most solemn hours I am ever likely to spend in my life.

I preached at Whippingham Church this evening (or should I say last evening) making such guarded reference as I could to the grave condition of the Queen.

Then I spent a quiet evening with the Clement Smith's[34] in the Rectory and at 11 went to bed. The latest news about the Queen had been that she was in much the same condition & that no immediate change was to be anticipated.

Just at midnight, a carriage was sent for me post haste with a letter saying that the R. Family wanted me to come at once and to remain in the house, the Queen being much worse.

34 Rev. Clement Smith, Chaplain in Ordinary to the Queen and Rector of St Mildred's Church, Whippingham, Isle of Wight.

I got into my clothes as fast as I could & got to the House at 12.20 but found I was not needed for the moment. Sir D. Powell, Sir James Reid, Edwards, Clinton, Bigge and Fritz Ponsonby were in council in Bigge's room & I joined them. They were at this moment in telephonic communication with Marlborough House.

They were discussing whether he [Prince of Wales] should not come at once as the Doctors thought the end not very far off. The poor Prince it seemed was worked up with all this travel in such stormy weather & under such strain & after much talk between Reid at this end & Knollys at the other end it was decided that the Prince & Emperor should start at 8 am tomorrow getting here in the forenoon. The Doctors think this will be in time.

Indeed they shrink from prophesying anything very decisively. But she has now become almost unconscious & has difficulty in swallowing. They were all glad I think that I had come to be in the house.

The men are all rather fagged out as they have literally & without exaggeration been telephoning & telegraphing without stop or stay for some 24 hours on end, including messages to the Colonies – to India – and to all the great offices in England.

After waiting about an hour we decided to go to our rooms, or such rooms as are available, for there are more people than beds, and await what may be wanted. I should like to have gone to some of the Princesses – (esp Princess Thora who arrived this afternoon) but I found they had given orders they would send for me when they wanted me to come, so I didn't like to press in.

And now I am just waiting & shall go presently to bed if they don't send.

It is a solemn moment in English History, or the History of the world, and the thoughts that rush in are overwhelming.

Dear old lady she is simply worn out after nearly 64 years of honest hard work for her people. How splendid that she should just end like this without even putting off her armour. God bless her.

I am so thankful to be here instead of at Holloway College! I should never have forgiven myself if when they wanted me at the close I had been far away & I do think my talks this afternoon were of some good.

It is so strange to find oneself in the midst of all the personal sorrow of a great family and also in the midst of the highest constitutional problems.

For example, if the Queen dies before the Prince starts from London, they say he could not start but must at once summon a Council as King & there are many more problems of a like sort which nobody is clear about for lack of any precedents within people's memory or knowledge. It does give one suggestive thoughts about national life and its meaning.

Now it is past two o'clock & as no message has come for me & all seems quiet in the house I shall go (again) to bed.

Ever Thine

R

Sir Frederick Ponsonby

The Bishop of Winchester retired to Whippingham Rectory and the others to their various houses. Bigge insisted on remaining and helping me to sit up all night to be instantly ready if any change should take place. I was to sit up until 6 a.m., when he would relieve me. I suggested his going up to my bedroom and lying down with rugs on the sofa. This he did, but it was already past one when he retired. I sat in the armchair in his writing-room and read, but at 4 a.m. I got so cold that I had to get a rug. Everything seemed ghostly and still, but curiously enough I did not seem at all sleepy. As I sat there I thought of all the people crowded into Osborne House and what the Queen's death would mean to them, what would happen when the Prince of Wales came to the throne, and what changes he would make. Gloomy thoughts in the small hours of the morning with only myself and a few policemen awake. At six Bigge turned up without my having to wake him and we had a cup of tea. I then retired to bed and slept till 9.30.

Cosmo Lang, Vicar of Portsea

It has been an anxious Sunday.

Monday, 21 January

Randall Davidson, Bishop of Winchester

I went down and found the house quiet and that the Queen had decidedly rallied. The servants said they had heard she was much better. I could find no one else and had to wait until 9 o'clock when it turned out that this was greatly exaggerated.

Sir James Reid

Was up all night with the Queen, Powell was with me, and we gave her oxygen frequently. We thought she was perhaps going to die quickly, but we did not fetch any of the Princesses, who never came to enquire at night.

Towards morning however, she rallied, and got stronger though was still almost unconscious until late in the morning, when she became more clear headed, and was able to speak and to swallow better.

Barlow arrived at 10, and at once saw the Queen with Powell and me, but could do nothing more, though we were very glad to have him with us.

Bulletin – Osborne, 21 January, 11 a.m.

The Queen has slightly rallied since mid-night. Her Majesty has taken more food and has had some refreshing sleep. There is no further loss of strength. The symptoms that give rise to most anxiety are those which point to a local obstruction in the brain circulation.

JAMES REID, M.D.
R. DOUGLAS POWELL, M.D.
THOMAS BARLOW, M.D.

Randall Davidson, Bishop of Winchester

During the morning she brightened up and said to Sir James Reid '*Am I better at all?*' He said '*Yes*', and then she eagerly answered '*Then may I have Turi?*' (her little Pomeranian dog). Turi was sent for, and she eagerly held him on the bed for about an hour.

Sir James Reid

To his wife, Susan

Bipps [the Queen] was very bad last night, and we thought she was going to bat [die]: but she has rallied and is rather better again! Come up to the bicycle house about 12.45 and I'll come to you.

George, Duke of York

Left Victoria by special train with Papa,[35] William,[36] uncle Arthur[37] & aunt Louise[38] for Portsmouth. Crossed over in 'Alberta' & reached Osborne at 11.20.

Sir Frederick Ponsonby

When I came down I found somewhat better news about the Queen; the Prince of Wales had returned, and the German Emperor had arrived. Although the rest of the Royal Family seemed to resent his coming and no one had asked him to come, he behaved in a most dignified and admirable manner. He said to the Princesses, '*My first wish is not to be in the light, and I will return to London if you wish. I should like to see Grandmamma before she dies, but if that is impossible I shall quite understand*'. Nothing could have been better.

Sir James Reid

The Prince of Wales, the Kaiser, the Duke of Connaught and the Duke of York arrived in the forenoon, and I took them all in separately to look at the Queen from the foot of the bed, but I did not then think it advisable for any of them to speak to her or to rouse her. The Queen's eyesight had for some time been so bad that there was no fear of her seeing them, even if she opened her eyes.

35 Prince of Wales.

36 Emperor of Germany.

37 Duke of Connaught.

38 Duchess of Connaught.

George, Duke of York

Thank God we found that darling Grandmama had rallied since last night & that her strength was still maintained.

The doctors allowed me to go in & see her, she looked just the same, not a bit changed, she was almost asleep & had her eyes shut, I kissed her hand, Motherdear was with me.

Sir Frederick Ponsonby

The whole house was crammed and even all the houses in the vicinity were full. I expected every minute to be turned out of my bedroom, which was large and comfortable, but no one even suggested this.

New York Times

The palace is packed. There is scarcely room for the Emperor of Germany and his staff. The accommodations are so severely taxed that the Battenberg children slept at Viscount Gort's[39] residence, East Cowes Castle, and the royal yachts at Cowes are being fitted up for the accommodation of visitors.

The Times

This has been a day of many arrivals and of faintly reviving hope. The Queen, as the first bulletin of this morning, issued at 11 o'clock, showed, rallied enough after midnight to be able to take some nourishment and to have some refreshing sleep; and it was announced that her strength this morning had not been

39 John Vereker, 5th Viscount Gort, owner of East Cowes castle.

diminished. This opportunity, it is said, was taken by the members of the Royal Family at Osborne, who had been in the Queen's bedroom before, to obtain some of the sleep of which they had been sadly in need.

LONDON

The Times

A special train, officially requisitioned, was kept under steam at Victoria Station last night in readiness to convey Ministers to Osborne, should their attendance be required.

Daily Express

Down in the docks, the latest rumours flew up and down the long quays. Men wheeling crates shouted them to men stacking timber, and men at the hatchways shouted them to men in the hold. In Wapping Wall at midday, four men tramped into a waterside tavern. They looked like workers from one of the neighbouring wharves, out for their dinner half-hour. '*Ere's God save her, mates!*' said one and he raised his tankard. '*God save her!*' said the other three. Without another word, the four rough Englishmen tramped out.

To the Editor of The Times

Sir, – As the news with regard to her Majesty is so serious, may I ask if the authorities will cause the bulletins to be exhibited in all post-offices (town and country), as they were when the Prince of Wales had his serious illness in 1871?
Your obedient servant,
G.R.T.

Lord Gower

The papers are full of the dangerous state of the Queen. I wired to Lorne [Duke of Argyll] this morning; an answer has just come from him '*Much worse*' so one fears what one dreads to think of.

Arthur Merrill

A Canadian publisher and author, who in collaboration with Rev. Henry Northrup published an 'instant' biography of Queen Victoria shortly after her death in 1901.

About one o'clock rival journals came out with display bills, each telling a totally different story of the state of the Queen's health in huge letters. On one was '*Queen Unconscious, Sinking Fast.*' These were green display bills. Others, yellow and white, also in huge lettering, read, '*Queen Rallying: Has Eaten and Slept. Official.*' What is more, the boys yelled out the two versions at the top of their voices. It was good for business, as each sold the papers in equal amount, the public being forced to buy both in order to try to make up its mind which was right.

The Mall in front of the Prince of Wales house was simply blocked from eleven o'clock on with callers anxious to sign their names in the book which lies inside the gates of the small, twelve foot square office. Hundreds had already signed by the middle of the day and thousands will have penned their names before the day has closed. It was a new book of red morocco. One of the royal servants stood over it, and when any signer showed a disposition to waste space remarked, '*Write close, please.*'

At the Garrick Club there was much discussion as to what should be done. It was taken for granted that the theatres would be closed for at least a week, and should the death be announced in the midst of a performance the houses would be forthwith closed. People were beginning to speculate as to the results.

Trades people were in an awful state of mind. There was no season last year, owing to the war, and now in blank despair they realise that there will be no season this year.

Bond street, Regent street, and Dover street are a sight to behold. Fashionable women are running and rushing about to their dressmakers countermanding coloured costumes which they had ordered for the coming spring season and imploring the modistes to turn out mourning gowns with the utmost rapidity.

Hatters are laying in a stock of deep hat bands, and stationers are getting mourning edged stationery, while crape is being ordered by the ton. As many orders are being booked each day as previously in six months, and the rush is tremendous.

London is just beginning to realise what the effects are of such a calamity as that of which everyone is prepared to hear at any moment.

OSBORNE HOUSE

George, Duke of York

Lunched in Durbar room. In afternoon, quite mild, walked with Papa, Motherdear, William, aunt Louise & uncle Arthur, we first went down to Osborne pier & then to East Cowes & paid a visit to James' convalescent home, where there were 15 soldiers back from South Africa. Had a talk to Bigge after tea. Wrote some letters.

Sir James Reid

In the afternoon I saw the Kaiser who was most anxious to know about his grandmother, and thanked me for my telegram which he said had at once decided him to come. I told him that I was anxious he should see the Queen alone, and talk to her, and promised to do my best to manage it, for which he thanked me, as it was the one thing he desired, saying he had a good report to her of his mother, etc., and that he would say nothing to excite her.

Randall Davidson, Bishop of Winchester

Throughout the day I did not go to the Queen's Room at all. I saw most of the members of the Family, either together or separately, and they all talked quietly over the position of matters.

It was arranged that I should stay at Kent House, Princess Victoria of Schleswig-Holstein [Thora] was there also. She and I had a great deal of conversation in the afternoon. She had been with the Queen for many weeks. The Queen had talked pretty often lately about illness and even death, which was not according to her wont.

'*When I was young I did so hate "religious" books. Now it is quite different. I feel to want & to like something of the kind*'.

'*Why did Christle when he was dying want the Holy Communion? I wonder if he really did or if they "got" him to have the service*'. Princess Thora assured her it was what he would always have wished & would certainly have asked for.

'*Well. I don't feel at all sure that I should wish for it just then. But I should like to have prayers*'.

And then, most delicious and characteristic of all (but this is quite private!) '*My dear, do you know I sometimes feel that when I die I shall be a little just a little nervous about meeting Grandpapa for I have taken to doing a good many things that he would not quite approve of.*'

Isn't that a beautiful and characteristic bit of herself, the simplicity of fault & expectation.

Bulletin – Osborne, 21 January, 5 p.m.

The slight improvement of this morning is maintained.
JAMES REID, M.D.
R. DOUGLAS POWELL, M.D.
THOMAS BARLOW, M.D.

Sir James Reid

In the evening I took the Prince of Wales to see the Queen and to speak to her.

Sir Frederick Ponsonby

When the Prince of Wales went in to see the Queen she became conscious for a moment and recognized him. She put out her arms and said '*Bertie*', whereupon he embraced her and broke down completely.

Sir James Reid

After the Prince of Wales left the Queen, Mrs Tuck and I went to her bedside, and H.M. took my hand and repeatedly kissed it. She evidently in her semi-conscious state did not realise the Prince had gone, and thought it was his hand she was kissing. Mrs Tuck, realising this, asked her if she still wanted the Prince of Wales, and she said '*yes*'. The Prince returned to her bedside and spoke to her and she said to him '*Kiss my face*'. Later on I took the Princess of Wales to see the Queen and left them together for a short time.

George, Duke of York

Family dinner at 8.30. Talked to Papa & Francis [Knollys]. Darling Grandmama rather better tonight, Motherdear saw her, she recognised her & talked to her, Papa also saw her this evening.

Randall Davidson, Bishop of Winchester

11.30pm
Kent House
My beloved Wife.
Again, in the middle of the night I send you a few lines.

I have just come back to 'Kent House' where I am staying tonight (and onwards) from dining in Osborne House.

I have had a full talk with the three doctors Reid, Powell & Barlow quietly in their own room. I asked them what store they really set by the improved bulletin.

'*Well, there is no doubt there is some definite rally & that there is more "recognition" & more "life"*'.

'*Tell me then, if it were the care of a Mrs Smith in Sloane St. & you were consulting over her, what prospect would you entertain or give to others?*'

They hesitated a good deal. Reid declined, from lack of general experience, to reply. At last Powell said, '*I should expect her perhaps to live for four or five days*' and after some discussion, Barlow agreed. Both were emphatic of course in saying that they could not prophesy and that it is perfectly possible that at any time some new complication may arise and bring about the end in an hour: and that it is also possible though very improbably that she might hold her own so strongly as to come back for a time to a sort of vegetable life.

The question arose whether I might safely sleep tonight at Kent House, with a fair assurance that there would not probably be any sudden termination before I could be sent for. They were all three emphatic that that is most unlikely, and that in any case there would almost certainly be a comatose period giving more than ample time to send for me. So, I am going to bed here in Kent House & am going to Osborne to breakfast.

After seeing the Doctors, I had a very long talk with the German Emperor & the Duke of Connaught (together). The Emperor is as nice on this occasion as anybody could be totally sinking his 'bossy' style & reiterating to the whole family that he is here as the Queen's grandson & not as Emperor & will do just what they would like him to do. I think he has even won over the hostile princesses to his side.

The Emperor and the Duke were both most keen to know what judgement we had formed about the probabilities!! I pointed out that our judgement didn't matter much, but told them, what the Doctors had said.

We then discussed what it might mean both personally & politically if the Q. were to be going on with a bare modicum of life.

The Duke very naturally clung to all possible hopefulness & would like her to 'remain alive' anyhow. He was like an honest simple schoolboy. The Emperor on the other hand was (again characteristically) full of the terribleness of a life that is no real life and spoke with splendid enthusiasm about the Queen's greatness for 63 years and his wish that there might be no 'mean or unfitting' physical close. He poured out really rather eloquently his views on to what a glorious life the Queen's had been, how early her greatness had begun, how undiminished it is even now & so on.

He compared her to 'Grandpapa' and said that 'Grandpapa' & the Queen were both lives of iron & that when iron is broke it doesn't waste away but 'goes crack'. Grandpapa had simply drawn to a worthy close his great life, the collapse coming when he heard that his 'great nephew' Prince of Baden had died. *'Exactly like Grandmama and Christle'.*

Altogether our talk was most interesting. He is a striking fellow, let people say what they will.

The Duke of Connaught spoke warmly of the good of my being here with them all and tried (not very successfully) to describe to the Emperor the accumulated offices I have as Bishop and otherwise.

Thine

R.

Bulletin – Osborne, 21 January, Midnight:

There is no material change in the Queen's condition. The slight improvement of the morning has been maintained throughout the day. Food has been taken fairly well, and some tranquil sleep secured.
JAMES REID, M.D.
R. DOUGLAS POWELL, M.D.
THOMAS BARLOW, M.D

London

Henry James

American author who had moved to England in 1869. Writing to Clare Benedict, his friend and fellow American, who was travelling around Europe with her mother Clara.

Reform Club
Dearest Benedicts.
To proceed immediately to the point, the poor dear old stricken Queen is *rapidly* dying and by the time this reaches you will probably be no more.

Blind, used up, utterly sickened and humiliated by the war, which she hated and deplored from the first (it's what has finished her) she is a very pathetic old monarchical figure.

It is a simple running down of the old used-up watch and no winding-up can keep for more than from hour re hour. As I write she is reported as 'rallying' a little, but it can only mean a postponement of a few hours.

I feel as if her death will have consequences in and for this country that no man can foresee.

The Prince of Wales is an arch-vulgarian (don't repeat this from me), the wretched little 'Yorks' are less than nothing; the Queen's magnificent duration had held things magnificently – beneficently – together and prevented all sorts of accidents. Her death, in short will let loose incalculable forces for possible ill. I am very pessimistic.

The Prince of Wales, in sight of the throne, and nearly 60, is 'carrying on' with Mrs. George Keppel, in a manner of the worst omen for the dignity of things. His accession in short is ugly and makes all for vulgarity and frivolity.

There will be tremendous obsequies, of course, even if they take place at Windsor, and not at the Abbey, as the nation will wish. (She has probably arranged to be placed at Frogmore with her husband – 'Frogmore' for the Empress of India!!) and probably for a year's mourning. Wear it you, too (as good Americans ought, for she was always nice to us), for a month. Forgive this unsightly scrawl to catch the post ...

Act II

The Angel of Death

22 January 1901

Tuesday, 22 January

Osborne House

Bulletin – Osborne, 22 January, 8 a.m.

The Queen this morning shows signs of diminishing strength, and her Majesty's condition again assumes a more serious aspect.
JAMES REID, M.D.
R. DOUGLAS POWELL, M.D.
THOMAS BARLOW, M.D.

Sir James Reid

Was up all night; I fetched Powell and Barlow repeatedly, but remained myself the whole time. The Queen was semi-conscious, her swallowing was difficult and tracheal rales were beginning. Her cough was efficient at first, but getting weaker and ineffective towards morning. I gave oxygen repeatedly. She took a little fluid food occasionally, with difficulty in swallowing. She knew and asked for me frequently.

About 9.30 a.m., when I had gone to my room for a short time to wash and change my clothes, and had asked Powell to go and take my place, he rushed up to my room, and asked me to hurry back as she looked like dying.

All the family were summoned.

Randall Davidson, Bishop of Winchester

Soon after 8 a.m., I was summoned from Kent House, a carriage being sent to bring me as quickly as possible to Osborne.

I went straight to the Queen's room. The Family were assembling, some of them not fully dressed. They knelt round the bed, the Prince of Wales on the Queen's right, the German Emperor on her left. About 10 or 12 others were there. The Queen was breathing with difficulty and moving somewhat restlessly. The nurse[1] was kneeling behind her in the bed, holding up the pillows. The three doctors were present. Although the Queen's breathing was so difficult she clearly was quite conscious. Ministry was difficult with so many persons in the room, some of them giving way a good deal to emotion.

Sir James Reid

The Bishop of Winchester said prayers for the dying while I kept plying her with oxygen. The Princesses Christian [Helena], Louise, and Beatrice kept telling her who was beside her (the Queen too blind to see), mentioning each other's names and those of all the rest of the family present, but omitting the name of the Kaiser who was standing at her bedside. I whispered to the Prince of Wales, '*Wouldn't it be well to tell her that her grandson the Emperor is here too.*' The Prince turned and said to me, '*No it would excite her too much*', so it was not done.

George, Duke of York

We were all sent for to darling Grandmama's room & we all thought the end was coming, but she rallied in a wonderful way

1 Nurse Mary Ann Soal, who was awarded the Gold Medal after the completion of her training at the Royal Free Hospital, London. She joined the Royal Household and was personal nurse to Queen Victoria from 1899.

& became better, so we all left her. This is indeed a terribly anxious time. I sent for May[2] [Duchess of York, who had remained in London] to come at once. Went for a short walk with Papa.

Sir James Reid

I sent out all the family to let her rest. She began to take food again, talked better and got clearer in her head, and I could not help admiring her clarity.

I went to tell the Kaiser I meant to take him to see the Queen when none of the family was there. He was very grateful and said, '*Did you notice this morning that everybody's name in the room was mentioned to her except mine*.' I replied, '*Yes, and that is one reason why I specially wish to take you there.*'

I went to the Prince of Wales to report about the Queen, and said I would like to take the Kaiser to see her. He replied, '*Certainly, and tell him the Prince of Wales wishes it.*' I took the Kaiser to see her, and sent all the maids out and took him up to the bedside, and said, '*Your Majesty, your grandson the Emperor is here; he has come to see you as you are so ill*', and she smiled and understood. I went out and left him with her five minutes alone. She said to me afterwards, '*The Emperor is very kind.*'

She does not look like dying just now; and I can't help admiring her determination not to give up the struggle while she can. I hardly dare to hope she may yet win, though she deserves to.

She often smiles when she hears my voice and says she will do '*anything I like*'. The whole thing is most pathetic, and rather gives me a lump in the throat!

2 Princess Victoria Mary of Teck, Duchess of York, *May* (1867–1953). Granddaughter-in-law. Age 33. Eldest daughter of the Duke of Teck. At the end of 1891 she was engaged to Albert Victor, Duke of Clarence, the eldest son of the Prince of Wales and second in line to the throne, who died suddenly from pneumonia in January 1892. In July the following year, she was married to his brother Prince George, Duke of York.

Bulletin – Osborne, 22 January, 12 o'clock:

There is no change for the worse in the Queen's condition since this morning's bulletin. Her Majesty has recognized the several members of the Royal Family who are here.
The Queen is now asleep.
JAMES REID, M.D.
R. DOUGLAS POWELL, M.D.
THOMAS BARLOW, M.D.

Sir Frederick Ponsonby

As the last death of a sovereign had occurred in 1837, no one seemed to know what the procedure was. We spent the evening looking up what had been done when George IV and William IV had died.

LONDON

Reginald Brett, Viscount Esher

The ignorance of historical precedent in men whose business it is to know is wonderful.

Almeric Fitzroy

The news that reached us so clearly pointed to an early and fatal end of the Queen's illness, that I thought it necessary to ask the Duke of

Norfolk[3] to let me see some representative of the Heralds' College without delay, relative to their part in the accession ceremonies.

I was thus able to turn to the examination of the precedents more directly affecting our own action. These unfortunately were not as full as we could have wished; our own records were in some respects at variance with, and in others did not confirm the notices in the 'Gazette', while printed accounts for which more or less authenticity was claimed differed from both.

Randall Davidson, Bishop of Winchester

The Queen's own diary about her own first Council meeting was the best guide they had for knowing what to do for the new King.

Almeric Fitzroy

I saw Spencer Ponsonby[4] the first thing this morning, with a view to having everything ready at St. James's Palace in the event of it being selected as the place for the Accession Council.

On reaching Whitehall I found that Mr. Balfour [First Lord of the Treasury], who had been told overnight to expect a summons to Osborne at any minute (to which end a special train was kept at Victoria with steam up all night), was still in Downing Street, and I therefore went across to urge upon him to obtain the earliest possible instructions if, as seemed inevitable, the Queen should not survive the day.

He was still at breakfast – 12.30 – though intending to start immediately afterwards; but, with his usual pleasantness and

3 Henry Fitzalan-Howard, 15th Duke of Norfolk. As hereditary Earl Marshal, he took responsibility for organising major ceremonial state occasions, having already organised the state funeral of William Gladstone in 1898.

4 Sir Spencer Ponsonby-Fane, sixth son of the 4th Earl of Bessborough. Comptroller of the Lord Chamberlain's Office and a first-class cricketer, playing for both Middlesex and Surrey.

accessibility, saw me at once, and promised to do his best to obtain prompt information for us.

Reginald Brett, Viscount Esher

A. J. B. [Balfour] left at two to-day for Osborne. Ritchie, the Home Secretary, is, apparently, not wanted.

When Harcourt[5] was Home Secretary [1880–85], the Queen sent him through [Henry] Ponsonby an instruction that at her death her successor should not be present at the Public Proclamation, a ceremonial that '*had been peculiarly painful to her.*' I told Douglas of this paper, and it was found at the Home Office last night and handed to Arthur Balfour who will show it to the Prince.

I saw the Duke of Norfolk, and arranged with him exactly what steps are to be taken, if, as Earl Marshal, he has to conduct the funeral.

The Lord Chancellor and the Speaker had put their heads together, and arranged that they would ignore the Council, and sit at once in their respective houses to take the oath of allegiance, forgetting that it is the Lord Chancellor who administers the oath at the Council to the Sovereign, and that the Sovereign must take the oath before anyone is justified in swearing allegiance.

No one seems to have taken the trouble to look even at the Annual Register, to ascertain what took place when William IV died.

What a series of political and social changes this event will produce! It is like beginning to live again in a new world.

Almeric Fitzroy

There was some uncertainty as to the preparation of the Speech the new Sovereign has to make to the Council. It was in this connection that Lord Salisbury had been consulted by the Duke of

5 Sir William Harcourt, Liberal statesman and former Leader of the Opposition.

Devonshire some weeks before, and delivered the astonishing opinion that the declaration made by the Queen in 1837 appeared to require very little change, and the Duke had to point out that at least two-thirds of it were quite inappropriate, and that the remainder required revision.

Reginald Brett, Viscount Esher

To Sir William Harcourt

The Prince of Wales has telegraphed to say that the end is near. If the Queen dies to-night, the Council will be held at St. James's Palace to-morrow. The question of uniform is undetermined at present.

Loulou[6] told me of Ponsonby's letter to you of which nothing was known. It was found at the H.O. [Home Office] last night, and Arthur [Balfour] took it to Osborne an hour ago.

Ritchie[7] is not sent for, has been at Eastbourne all along, and apparently is not wanted!

I cannot describe to you the ignorance, the historical ignorance, of everyone from top to bottom – who should know something of procedure. You would think that the English Monarchy had [not] been buried since the time of Alfred.

There has been a great rush to get everything ready, but we are in smoother water to-day. The Queen has had a return to consciousness and has recognised her children, but still there seems to be no hope of any strong revival, so that the end will be a release. It is really merciful that her illness has been so short. You know well what endless confusion is already created by the accumulation of documents for signature, some of the Judges even have been unable to proceed on the Assize for want of the Queen's authority.

6 Lewis Harcourt, son of Sir William Harcourt, he was to become Secretary of State for the Colonies under Asquith.

7 Charles Ritchie, Home Secretary.

What changes, political and social, this event will produce! The idea is that it will be impossible to escape from a great national demonstration of respect and sorrow in London.

No one knows yet what the Queen's own wishes may be upon that point.

OSBORNE HOUSE

Sir James Reid

For about three hours she was left comparatively alone with the maids and nurse, I looking in and out occasionally. During this time she asked for Mr Smith of Whippingham, who was sent for. I helped to lift and move her when necessary, as the maids said she liked me to do it. She was again getting weaker, and at about 1.45 she got very bad again and at 3 we summoned the family once more.

Sir Frederick Ponsonby

We heard the Queen was sinking and I sent for Bigge and Edwards. A carriage was sent for the Bishop of Winchester and Clement Smith, the Rector of Whippingham.

Randall Davidson, Bishop of Winchester

While we were at luncheon about 2.15 I was summoned to go at once, and Clement Smith came also. We found her much weaker and the Family again assembled.

The Princess of Wales was with her and holding her up. The Emperor also was making himself most useful to Doctors and Family. They were administering oxygen to relieve her breathing – rather a cumbersome process.

We remained in the room a long time, Clement Smith and I saying prayers and hymns at intervals. She was not obviously responsive to the words said, but certain things, and specially the last verse of '*Lead, Kindly Light*' seemed at once to catch her attention, and she showed that she followed it.

So long thy power hath blessed me, sure it still
Will lead me on,
O'er moor and fen, o'er crag and torrent, till
The night is gone;
And with the morn those angel faces smile,
Which I have loved long since, and lost awhile.

Sir James Reid

The Bishop and Mr Smith kept alternately reciting prayers and verses of Scripture, but she still lingered on, and, after a time, as it was necessary to make her comfortable, I asked the family to go out again, the Princesses going to her sitting room, and the Prince of Wales and Princes, into the Prince Consort's room to write telegrams and talk.

During this time I asked the Prince of Wales whether it would not be better to suspend the prayers until the Queen was actually dying, as it was otherwise so painful, and he said, '*Certainly, tell him not to come into the room until I send for him.*'

Randall Davidson, Bishop of Winchester

I remained in the Dressing Room and in the adjoining Drawing Room. There I had a good deal of talk with the Emperor, who was full of touching loyalty to 'Grandmamma' as he always described her. '*She has been a very great woman. Just think of it: she remembers George III, and now we see in the Twentieth Century. And all that time what a life she has led. I have never been with her without feeling that she was in every sense my Grandmamma and made me love her as such. And yet the minute we began to talk about political things she made me feel we were equals and could speak as Sovereigns. Nobody had such power as she.'* I spoke of the good his coming to England would do. He said repeatedly, *'My proper place now is here; I could not be away.'*

Sir Frederick Ponsonby

Arthur Balfour arrived. He was astounded at the accumulation of official Boxes that had taken place during the last week and said it showed what a mass of routine work the Queen had to do. Still there was the point to be considered how the machine could go on without her. Judges, for instance, could not function without a warrant signed by her: all sorts of appointments could not be made without her sanction. He impressed on Bigge the necessity for summoning a Privy Council, no matter what happened. But we all knew it was only a matter of hours.

Bulletin – Osborne, 22 January, 4 p.m.

The Queen is slowly sinking.
JAMES REID, M.D.
R. DOUGLAS POWELL, M.D.
THOMAS BARLOW, M.D.

Sir James Reid

I returned to her room after five minutes absence and did not leave. The family returned soon after me, and kept going in and out.

I [was] kneeling at her right side with my right hand on her right pulse, my left arm supporting her in a semi upright position, helped by the Kaiser who knelt on the opposite side of the bed. The Prince of Wales was sitting behind me at the end, and Princess Louise kneeling on my right. All the rest were round about, Nurse Soal sitting on the bed at the top, and Mrs Tuck standing beside her.

The Queen kept looking at me, and frequently gasped '*Sir James*', and '*I'm very ill*' and I each time replied, '*Your Majesty will soon be better.*'

Sir Thomas Barlow

The daylight was passing and a few candles and a lamp were lit. The day might have been in September. There wasn't a trace of winter gloom. There was scarcely a sound but that of a fountain in the Bower garden close by.

The Queen's bedroom was a little bigger than your large bedroom. The Queen lay on a simple, narrow mahogany bedstead with a quite small dark chocolate coloured canopy at the head. The furniture otherwise was quiet enough, mahogany chairs and a wardrobe. The walls were covered with pictures, the largest of them of sacred subjects, and some portraits of the Prince Consort and others.

The Queen's illness was really a failure of the vessels of the brain – not an apoplexy exactly but probably the arteries of the brain getting slowly damaged, especially in the part corresponding with the centre for speech and the portion controlling the right side of the face. Beyond this there was no actual paralysis till the vital powers began to fail and she gradually sank, [although] her utterance was hampered, she understood everything that was said.

The Prince of Wales and the Royal Dukes, Princess Christian [Helena] and Princess Henry [Beatrice] were also kneeling at the bedside and the Duke and Duchess of Connaught, the Duc[hess] of Saxe-Coburg [widow of Prince Alfred] and most of the grandchildren.

The most interesting of the bystanders was the Prince of Wales who sat and knelt to the right of the bed and the Emperor [Kaiser], who stood near the Queen's left shoulder. The Prince of Wales full of tenderness, now and then telling her about each in turn.

But the Emperor's was the figure that to us was the most striking personality in the room next to the Queen. There he stood with his eyes immovably fixed on his grandmother, apparently with no thought but of her. When asked to speak he said he had come to tell her about the Empress Frederick, that she was a little better, she was taking drives again, that she sent her love, and then quietly, he took his place of watching again no self-consciousness or posing there but simple dignity and intense devotion.

But in the earlier part of the day, when the family had been summoned he had showed himself so ready and deft in putting in a pillow here and there and when some of the others said 'more air' he was away to the window to lift it himself if I had not forestalled him.

The Bishop of Winchester and Mr. Clement Smith were in the room at times and recited passages of the Bible and a few collects and hymns – Abide with me, Lead kindly light, Rock of Ages.

At least three times in the day the family were assembled, expecting she was going.

The last waiting time continued I should think, an hour – the breathing got shallow. When the very end came it was without any struggle, a gentle fading away.

There was the poor Queen not suffering much as far as we could judge but sinking by slow degrees, her splendid constitution showing itself to the last, so that her pulse held up till just before she died.

She was, I believe, conscious till quite a short time before she passed away, for as each son and daughter and grandchild was spoken of and kissed her hand she showed signs of recognition and she even mentioned their names more or less clearly. Her speech which had been impaired seemed really to brighten on the last day of her life. She had been able to make us understand her likes and dislikes and her wishes in monosyllables and said in few words though not complete sentences. But on the last day she clearly understood well and said the children's names without trouble.

About an hour before she died, she had not seen the Duchess of York and several times asked for May, and when the Duchess came she recognised her.

Randall Davidson, Bishop of Winchester

At 6 o'clock we were told that the end was certainly approaching, but the breathing was so laboured that ministry was difficult or impossible. Then came a great change of look and complete calmness. I had been mainly in the Dressing Room. At 6.25 Powell summoned me to come in. I said the Commendatory Prayer and one or two texts and the Aaronic blessing

Sir Thomas Barlow

Her face was quite beautiful in its way; she had but little pain; her expression was for the most part calm. There was a simple dignity like that of an old Roman. The good dressers were round her, and a devoted nurse who has worked at the Cottage Hospital here was kneeling at the back of the bed and holding the Queen as only a human body can support a sick person. Sir James Reid knelt down by the bedside and had one arm also supporting the Queen's back. He had tended her so long and faithfully it was fitting that he should support her to the last. The Princess of Wales was on one side holding her hand and Princess Louise on the other holding the other.

Sir James Reid

A few minutes before she died her eyes turned fixedly to the right and gazed on the picture of Christ in the 'Entombment of Christ' over the fireplace.

Princess Helena

I shall never forget the look of radiance on her face at last when she opened her dear eyes quite wide & one felt & knew she saw beyond the Border Land & had seen & met all her loved ones.

George, Duke of York

I shall never forget that scene in her room, with all of us sobbing & heartbroken round her bed.

Sir James Reid

Her pulse kept beating well till the end when she died with my arm round her. I gently removed it, let her down on the pillow, and kissed her hand before I got up.

When all was over most of the family shook hands with me and thanked me by the bedside, and the Kaiser also squeezed my hand in silence. I told the Prince of Wales to close her eyes.

Queen Victoria

I die in peace with all, fully aware of my many faults, relying with confidence on the love, mercy and goodness of my Heavenly Father and His Blessed Son and earnestly trusting to be reunited to my beloved Husband, my dearest Mother, my loved Children and 3 dear sons-in-law. And all who have been very near and dear to me on earth. Also I hope to meet those who have so faithfully and so devotedly served me, especially good John Brown[8] and good Annie Macdonald.[9]

Randall Davidson, Bishop of Winchester

We left the Family alone for a few minutes. Then the King came out alone. I was in the passage and was the first to greet him as Sovereign. I then went to the Equerries' Room, where Clarendon[10] (Lord Chamberlain), Arthur Balfour, Sir Arthur Bigge, and (I think) Edwards, were present, and told them that the end had come.

Sir Frederick Ponsonby

The Duke of Argyll told me that the last moments were like a great three-decker ship sinking. She kept on rallying and then sinking.

Randall Davidson, Bishop of Winchester

In accordance with arrangements already made, the house was at once surrounded by police at intervals to prevent any servant or messenger from taking the tidings outside until telegrams had been despatched to the Prime Minister, the Lord Mayor, and several other potentates.

8 John Brown, the Queen's personal attendant from 1862 until his death in 1883.

9 Annie MacDonald, the Queen's principal dresser until her death in 1897.

10 Edward Villiers, 5th Earl of Clarendon. Lord Chamberlain of the Household.

King Edward VII

To the Lord Mayor of London

My beloved mother, the Queen, has just passed away, surrounded by her children and grandchildren.
ALBERT EDWARD

Randall Davidson, Bishop of Winchester

Then, after ten minutes or so, Inspector Fraser[11] took a message to the gate, where a crowd was waiting.

Bulletin – Osborne, 22 January, 6.45 p.m.

Her Majesty the Queen breathed her last at 6.30 p.m., surrounded by her children and grand-children
JAMES REID, M.D.
R. DOUGLAS POWELL, M.D.
THOMAS BARLOW, M.D.

11 Superintendent of the Household Police.

Act III

A Country in Mourning

22–24 January 1901

Tuesday Evening, 22 January

Osborne House

Sir Frederick Ponsonby

I was told the scene on the hill down to Cowes was disgraceful. Reporters in carriages and on bicycles were seen racing for the post office in East Cowes, and men were shouting as they ran, '*The Queen is dead*'.

The Times

From our Special Correspondent, Osborne
I cannot close this without a description of a very painful scene which is described only out of a sense of duty, and in obedience to an instinct of journalistic self-preservation.

It happened that I was not at the gates of the lodge when the news of the Queen's death was announced by Mr. Fraser, nor was there any object in being there, since the news was certain to be received in London; in fact, it was received some minutes before it could be received at the gates. They are about a quarter of a mile from the house, and it was certain that the telegraph from the house to London would be quicker than human transmission from the house to the gate.

But a few moments after the news had been made known at the gate I was driving up the York Avenue to Osborne in obedience to the summons, and in ignorance of the calamity which had befallen the nation, when I was apprised of it in a very shocking and unprecedented way. Loud shouts were heard in the distance, then came a crowd of carriages at the gallop, of bicycles careering down the hill at a breakneck speed, of runners bawling '*Queen dead*' at the top of their voices. The sound suggested a babel of cries at a foxhunt rather than the very solemn occasion which had called them forth; and it has to be confessed with shame that they were emitted by persons connected with the Press, although not, of course, with any London paper of long standing.

They were an outrage, and, taken in combination with a fictitious and disgraceful 'interview' with 'the Queen's physician' which has caused much pain and annoyance, they contribute a real danger to the better class of journalism, and, through it, to the public. How can journalists expect to be treated with consideration when, on an occasion so mournful, they behave in a manner so horribly contrary to common decency?

LONDON

Arthur Merrill

The Queen had died at half-past six in Cowes, and one hour later the Evening News had a black bordered special out on the street. The other papers followed with rapidity, and soon the St. James Gazette had out a special memorial number, selling like hot cakes.

The scene in the Strand by eight o'clock beggared description. At that time the people were driving down in shoals to the theatres. Bigger and bigger grew the numbers, until the Strand was blocked with carriages. Most of the theatres at once closed their gates, placing heavy black bordered notices outside to the effect that, owing to the death of the Queen, their performances were postponed until further notice. Those theatres leaving their doors open, which allowed would-be visitors to enter the hall, were sorry for it. After a very short time their box office clerks were pestered to death by all sorts of inquiries. Can you realise what London is without theatres? I never did myself until this evening, for not only was it those who came to see the performances who stood there in blank amazement, but also those who were to have given the performance.

In little or no time the Strand was crowded with members of the choruses, with paint still on their faces, actors with their make-up scarce off, musicians with their instruments, carpenters and scene shifters in their shirt sleeves, all not quite knowing what to do or where to go. Never, never has such a sight been seen before. It was quite unique.

The notices that were put up in front of the theatres telling of the postponement of the play were all very heavily bordered with black. These notices were ready last evening – aye, and the evening before for that matter.

Kitty Marion

Actress and prominent activist in the Women's Suffrage movement.

The manager of the Opera House, Cheltenham, announced to the audience the news of Queen Victoria's death. People listened and quietly dispersed. It seemed as if the world stood still and could never continue without the Queen. However, the following day King Edward VII was proclaimed King and life went on as usual.

Violet R. Markham

Writer and social reformer. The granddaughter of Sir Joseph Paxton, designer of the Crystal Palace.

In London little groups of people in the streets gathered together and sang God Save the Queen, perhaps of all the demonstrations the most spontaneous and moving.

Arthur Merrill

The cheap shops on the Strand promptly began to shut up, but before they did I noticed that several men's clothiers had promptly dressed their windows with black ties and mourning gloves, upon which forthwith there was a run, causing them to remain open later than they would have done otherwise.

Down Fleet street way the offices of the evening papers were besieged by leather-lunged newspaper venders, who fought each other in their anxiety to be first served, and to rush off to the West End.

Around St. Paul's the people rallied in their thousands. They had come to hear 'Big Tom' ring out, that great bell which, you must understand, has only once before rung out the death toll of royalty, which death was that of the Duke of Clarence. And toll it did, with impressive resounding and with the full force of sixteen tons of hollow metal, and just one minute between each great cavernous sounding rumble which filled out into volumes of sound.

Mary Monkswell

A Victorian diarist and wife of the Liberal politician Robert Collier, 2nd Baron Monkswell, who served briefly as Under-Secretary of State for War.

On this day at a quarter to nine, while we were sitting at dinner, the butler brought the news that our great Queen had departed this life. May she rest in peace.

Arthur Merrill

I passed on to the Mansion House. There was yet another great scene. Crowds and crowds, surging and swaying, special police everywhere trying to restrain the people who, all at the same time, wanted to read the bulletin telling of the death of the Queen, sent by the Prince of Wales fifteen minutes after her death.

Buses were crowded to overflowing with people who had made up their minds to see the town under its excitement from their tops. After all, what else was there to do? Not a place of amusement was open. Soon after this it commenced to rain, and then the people began to hurry down off the 'bus tops.'

Kate Frye

Katharine Parry Frye, actress, diarist and suffragist.

The Queen is Dead. We heard the paper boys in the street about nine o'clock. As I write the bells are tolling. The earth will be a very black place for a few weeks. I am about to undress for bed but stopped to write these few lines first.

George Gissing

A Yorkshire novelist, Man of Letters, and author of New Grub Street. *Writing to his son from Paris.*

My dear Walter,
News comes that the Queen is dead. I must send you a line, for when you are a man you will remember the death of Queen Victoria, & this letter which your father wrote to you. There will now be once more a King of England; let us hope he will do his duty as well as Queen Victoria did. Kings & Queens have not so much

power now as they used to have in the old days, but they can still do a great deal of harm if they are foolish or wicked. Queen Victoria always acted for the good of her country, & it is because the English people know she did so, that they grieve for her death. I am very much afraid that her life was shortened by the miserable war in South Africa, which she seems never to have approved. It is a sorrowful thing that her long reign, so full of good things, was not allowed to end in quietness, as she hoped.

OSBORNE HOUSE

Randall Davidson, Bishop of Winchester

I walked to Kent House and returned a little later, when I was sent for by the Prince and Princess of Wales (as they still wished to be called till the next day). They expressed a wish that we should have a little Service in the room beside the Queen's bed at 10 o'clock that night. I had a long talk with both. Then visited Princess Christian [Helena] and Princess Beatrice. They were both calm and sensible and discussed many details.

Sir James Reid

The Prince and Princess of Wales sent for me and thanked me together in their room, and the Prince said, '*You are an honest straightforward Scotchman*', and '*I shall never forget all you did for the Queen*'. The Princess cried much, shook hands and thanked me.

Sir Frederick Ponsonby

The Princess of Wales refused to be acknowledged as Queen and would not let anyone kiss her hand. She added that there could only be one Queen until the funeral and that she wished for the present to remain as Princess of Wales.

Sir James Reid

Later in the evening I went to see the Prince of Wales to remind him about the Queen's coffin. I found him in Edwards' room with the rest of the family, reading the Queen's written instructions about her funeral and other allied matters. It so happened that she mentioned that she wished her coffin to be made on the model of those in the Royal Vault at Windsor Castle (St George's Chapel), and on my telling the Prince that this was in the Lord Chamberlain's department, he told me to speak to Lord Clarendon, who was at Osborne (at East Cowes Castle) and fire the necessary orders. Accordingly, I wrote to Clarendon telling him that the coffin must be at Osborne on Thursday morning, so that the Queen's body might be put in it that day. I was very busy and tired.

Randall Davidson, Bishop of Winchester

The Household party at dinner was very large, and when dinner was half over I left with Arthur Balfour to secure a talk with him about the situation and also about some other urgent matters on which he thought conference desirable.

Sir James Reid

I was sent for, and left the dinner table to help the maids and nurse to arrange the Queen's body and to lift it to her usual bed, and replace the latter in its normal position. (She had a ventral hernia and a prolapse of the uterus.) I left them to dress her, and saw her later, looking beautiful, surrounded by loose flowers and palms strewn on the bed.

Randall Davidson, Bishop of Winchester

At 10.15 we all gathered in the Queen's Room and had a calm and bright little Service. She was lying in the bed where she had died, all being beautifully arranged, with quantities of white lace and a few simple flowers; the little crucifix which had always hung over her head within the bed being in her hand. They all, I think, liked our little Service.

I remained far on into the night talking over many details with Bigge and Arthur Balfour and Sir Francis Knollys. I also paid a long visit to Dr. Barlow in his room. Nobody could have been more sensible and helpful than he.

Lady Susan Reid

To her mother-in-law, Beatrice Reid

Everyone thinks it is wonderful what he has been to her all these years, and to know how she depended and clung to him to the last is so touching. When it was all over all the family came, one after the other, to Jamie to thank him for all he had done for his Queen. He said it was very touching. I fear the reaction after this great strain will be very trying and Jamie will feel his life so empty. I saw him for a few moments. He was very exhausted and worn out with the emotions of the day, but not harassed by thinking anything more could have been done. He has all the Queen's last wishes written down by her, so of course there is still much to do.

Sir Frederick Ponsonby

A Privy Council seemed urgent, but at first the Prince of Wales refused to go and argued there was no immediate hurry. When Lord Salisbury cyphered to Arthur Balfour that there must be no delay, the Prince consented to go to London.

London

Almeric Fitzroy

I made my way to Spencer Ponsonby about seven, and was with him when, at 7.10, a telephone message announced that all was over, the Queen having breathed her last in the majesty of perfect composure at 6.30.

It was necessary at once to survey the Banqueting Hall and see what arrangements would have to be made, and just as we were starting we met Pembroke,[1] who accompanied us. It was very dark, most of the caretakers were off duty, and in our efforts to reach the goal we were more than once baffled by locked doors. Indeed, we must have presented the appearance of conspirators as we threaded our way through the obscure purlieus of the Palace and at last emerged into the hall, the proportions of which were very dimly visible.

It was not till eight o'clock that I got away, and found Jack Sanders and the Privy Council Office messenger at my door, both of whom I had to dispose of before I could dress for dinner, and did not arrive at 78 Eaton Square till 8.30. I had hardly been at the table ten minutes when a box came from the Lord President[2] containing a letter from Knollys, with some of the information

1 Sidney Herbert, 14th Earl of Pembroke. Lord Steward of the Household.

2 Spencer Compton Cavendish, 8th Duke of Devonshire. Lord President of the Council.

we wanted, including the announcement that the royal style was to be Edward VII.

I was back in Whitehall by ten, and went over to the Foreign Office to see 'Pom' McDonnell[3] and Sanders; but it was not till eleven o'clock that we heard the Council was to be at 2 p.m. on the following day, and that all Privy Councillors were to be summoned.

For three further hours we were engaged perfecting our preparations, and by 2 a.m. I was able to go to bed satisfied that the order of business and the ceremonial arrangements were complete so far as I was concerned.

Wednesday, 23 January

Osborne

Court Circular

The Prince of Wales, the Duke of Connaught, the Duke of York, Prince Christian of Schleswig-Holstein, and the Duke of Argyll left Osborne this morning, crossing over to Portsmouth on board H.M.Y. Alberta.

The Lord Chamberlain and the Right Hon. A. J. Balfour have left Osborne.

Randall Davidson, Bishop of Winchester

I was at Osborne House early, in time to see Arthur Balfour and others before they started with the Prince of Wales for London.

The Prince left us directions to arrange the Dining Room as a sort of Mortuary Chapel in which the coffin might be placed next day.

3 Sir Schomberg McDonnell, Principal Private Secretary to Lord Salisbury.

I set to work on these arrangements with the Princesses. We telegraphed to London to Messrs Waring to send down instantly men with crimson hangings and many other things, so as completely to transform the room.

Sir James Reid

In the morning I saw the Queen's body and that all was nicely arranged. I took Powell and Barlow to the room to see her. I was busy in the forenoon with Powell and Barlow drawing up the report.

London

Caroline Holland

Daughter of Sir Henry Holland, her diaries were published posthumously as Notebooks of a Spinster Lady *in 1919.*

London looks very sad to-day. Already everyone in black; there is scarce a bit of colour to be seen. It was almost startling, when I went to luncheon at one o'clock in Eaton Square, to find Lord Knutsford[4] in gorgeous attire just starting to attend the first Privy Council of the new reign. The wording of the summons was from the King, but the official telegrams posted about the town stated that the Prince and Princess of Wales would arrive in London today. Although actually King, he is not so officially until he has issued the Proclamation giving his style and title, That will appear to-morrow, but numbers of people were gathered opposite St. James's Palace, expecting to see it posted to-day.

4 Henry Thurston Holland, 1st Viscount Knutsford and former Secretary of State for the Colonies. Half-brother to Caroline Holland.

Mary Monkswell

It seems to have taken place with such frightful rapidity, we are all quite stunned. Today, actually to-day, I saw Lord Ripon[5] in his uniform & Order of the Garter, start from No. 9 Chelsea Embankment, & at the same time Sir Mountstuart Grant Duff,[6] in his uniform, emerged from No. 11 Chelsea Embankment to go to the Privy Council meeting at St. James's Palace. Last night our dear Queen felt so close to us, but to-day so far off.

Caroline Holland

I went round to Marlborough House at twelve o'clock to inscribe my name. There was a constant flow of black-robed people pouring into the lodge where the Visitors' Book is kept. And all the while a little brown terrier and a black cat, in contrast to the general grief, were having a rollicking game of play, scrimmaging round and round the court, and tearing up the gravel beneath our feet. Someone called the attention of the policeman on duty to their pranks, but he only nodded benevolently and said; '*Oh, they are all right, they are old friends*.' From time to time a footman in magnificent livery stepped forward with a rake or broom to smooth down the havoc they had wrought.

The Royalties were expected, but there was such a crowd I was afraid to wait. I have since seen two people who say they did see the Prince arrive. One of them reports that he sat back in a closed brougham; the other that he was standing up in the carriage (most improbable!) bowing. Both accounts agree that he was received by the crowd with hats off, but no cheering.

5 George Robinson, 1st Marquess of Ripon.

6 Sir Mountstuart Grant Duff, former Under-Secretary of State for the Colonies.

Almeric Fitzroy

I looked in at St. James's Palace and saw to the final arrangements of the room, and it was not long before the Privy Councillors began to arrive, and it was plain we should have a big muster.

Reginald Brett, Viscount Esher

It was not held in the Throne Room but in the Banqueting Room. Everyone in uniform. There were about 150 people there. Some curious old fossils.

Almeric Fitzroy

At last the moment arrived when the Lord President, with the Royal Dukes, the Archbishop, the Prime Minister, and the Lord Chancellor, repaired to the King to announce the assembly of the Council.

On their return, after a few prefatory sentences from the Lord President, I read the Proclamation, which has a sustained stateliness of diction that makes it very impressive if properly delivered.

A prolonged wait then ensued for the signing of the Proclamation.

Reginald Brett, Viscount Esher

The ceremony was unimposing, but the King was very dignified. He spoke exceedingly well; began in a broken voice, but gathered strength as he proceeded.

King Edward VII

Your Royal Highnesses, My Lords, and Gentlemen, this is the most painful occasion on which I shall ever be called upon to address you.

My first and melancholy duty is to announce to you the death of My Beloved Mother the Queen, and I know how deeply you, the whole Nation, and I think I may say the whole world, sympathise with Me in the irreparable loss we have all sustained. I need hardly say that My constant endeavour will be always to walk in Her footsteps. In undertaking the heavy load which now devolves upon Me, I am fully determined to be a Constitutional Sovereign in the strictest sense of the word, and as long as there is breath in My body to work for the good and amelioration of My people.

I have resolved to be known by the name of Edward, which has been borne by six of My ancestors. In doing so I do not undervalue the name of Albert, which I inherit from My ever to be lamented, great and wise Father, who by universal consent, is I think deservedly known by the name of Albert the Good, and I desire that his name should stand alone.

In conclusion, I trust to Parliament and the Nation to support Me in the arduous duties which now devolve upon Me by inheritance, and to which I am determined to devote My whole strength during the remainder of My life.

Reginald Brett, Viscount Esher

Then a cushion was put at his right hand, and the Royal Dukes did homage. All knelt and kissed his hand, except the old Duke of Cambridge.[7] Then at his left hand another cushion was placed,

7 Prince George, Duke of Cambridge (1819–1904). Cousin to the Queen and grandson of George III. Age 81. A distinguished soldier and former Commander-in-Chief of the British Army, he had fought at the battles of Alma, Balaclava and Inkerman. Acknowledged to be a kind and considerate man.

and the Duke of Devonshire and Lord Salisbury, followed by others, performed the same ceremony. He raised Lord Salisbury very tenderly and respectfully.

John Wodehouse, Earl of Kimberley

Leader of the Liberals in the House of Lords.

The new King made an excellent short speech. As to the rest of the proceedings they can only be described as 'hugger mugger'. After the Ministers & a few others had taken the oath in the usual manner, the oath was administered to the rest in a body, but there was so much confusion that I could not make out exactly what was going on.

Almeric Fitzroy

The difficulty of swearing so many Privy Councillors was got over with less confusion than expected, and both Clarendon and Portland[8] said they never saw so large a function better arranged.

The Times

The Archbishop of York's[9] late arrival at the Privy Council meeting was due to the fact that his Grace only learnt the sad news of the Queen's death in Yorkshire on Wednesday morning, and that the train by which he hastened to town did not arrive in London until half an hour after the time which, unknown to him, had been fixed for the council. The Archbishop arrived at St James's Palace just as the Council was over, and only in time to sign the roll.

8 William Cavendish-Bentinck, 6th Duke of Portland. Master of the Horse.

9 William Maclagan, Archbishop of York.

Almeric Fitzroy

The King received me at Marlborough House the same afternoon, and was complimentary to everything except the pens, which might indeed have been described, in the vigorous language of William IV, as d---d bad.

My object in going to Marlborough House was to obtain the text of the King's declaration for publication in the 'Gazette,'[10] and I was rather disturbed to hear that no notes existed. This the King confirmed and seemed rather surprised that we had not made arrangements for his being adequately reported. Apart from the precedents which pointed to the new Sovereign having invariably made the declaration from a carefully prepared and written form, it was not easy to reconcile the presence of reporters with the character of the meeting; but the question for the moment was how to provide the text.

The King intimated that Lord Rosebery's[11] retentive memory might be brought into requisition, and added the suggestion that my memory was probably good enough to recall what he said.

It was easy to say that I had listened with great attention and been much impressed by His Majesty's remarks, but I confessed to some hesitation in assuming so grave a responsibility. However, the King was very pleasant about it, and I left undertaking to see that the difficulty should be surmounted somehow.

Two hours afterwards, while I was with the Lord President, Lord Suffield[12] and Arthur Balfour arrived: the former had recovered from the depths of Lord Rosebery's memory the main sequence of the sentences, and the King had made some revision of it in extremely illegible pencil marks. With this to work upon, I was able to restore the exordium and some other phrases which

10 The official journal of record since 1665.

11 Archibald Primrose, 5th Earl of Rosebery. Author and former Liberal Prime Minister.

12 Charles Harbord, Baron Suffield. A close friend and Lord-in-Waiting in Ordinary to the King.

I remembered had been used, and then from the Duke's dictation I wrote out a fair copy which both Arthur Balfour and Suffield agreed was as near the original as possible.

Mr. Balfour raised the point whether the King was correct in describing all the six Edwards as his ancestors. I maintained he was, as the term did not imply lineal descent so much as succession; and Lord Suffield thought the same. Later Suffield returned, having submitted the draft to the King, who was quite content with it; and the declaration has now taken its place among State documents of the highest interest and value.

George, Duke of Cornwall and York

Saw Holzmann,[13] about the Duchy of Cornwall, I have now succeeded Papa as the Duke of Cornwall. Both Houses of Parliament met. Uncle Arthur & I went to the House of Lords & took the Oath. Came home, busy answering letters & telegrams.

Osborne

Sir James Reid

At two o'clock I cycled to May Cottage for five minutes to see Susan and Margaret[14] whom I took to see the Queen.

Lady Susan Reid

I was allowed to see her lying on her bed – it was so beautiful. Her face like a lovely marble statue, no sign of illness or age, and

13 Sir Maurice Holzmann, secretary to the Duchy of Cornwall.

14 Margaret Spencer, sister of Susan Reid. Married to the Hon. Charles Spencer, later Viscount Althrop and 6th Earl Spencer.

she still looked 'the Queen', her wedding veil over her face and a few loose flowers on her bed – all so simple and grand. I shall never forget it!'

Randall Davidson, Bishop of Winchester

I had a long walk with Dr. Barlow and much interesting talk. Then a series of interviews with most of the Princesses and with the Queen, and then a long one with the Emperor. I paid a visit to the Queen's room. Nothing could be better than the simple arrangements in her room.

During the afternoon the servants and tenants were allowed to pass through the room and to see her as she lay.

At 6 o'clock we again had a Service in the room, at which most of the Family were present. It was, at their request, somewhat fuller than the Service of the previous evening.

Sir James Reid

Susan and Margaret staid till 6.40, when I went to the Queen's room with Fuchs[15] who came to make sketches. He was to have made a plaster cast of her face by the Kaiser's orders, but the Princesses were all against it and said the Queen would not have liked it.

I left him at 8.10, and told the maids that he was not to be left alone with the body, but that one of them must always be there unless I was. Pfyffer[16] was hanging about there too on the pretext

15 Emil Fuchs, an Austrian sculptor and fashionable artist living in London.

16 Secretary to the Kaiser.

of having charge of Fuchs. I told the maids that my order applied to him also.

Randall Davidson, Bishop of Winchester

Herr Fuchs, the sculptor, arrived having received permission to make a cast of the Queen's face. To this Queen Alexandra and the Princesses (rightly as I thought) objected most strongly, and, after some difficulty, succeeded in getting by telephone the King's sanction to there being drawings only and no cast. Herr Fuchs remained in the room nearly the whole night doing some admirable charcoal drawings.

In the evening [Waring's] men arrived, and in a marvellously short space of time all the transformations [to the dining room] was effected, that part of the room which was to be used as a Chapel being beautifully draped with crimson from ceiling to floor, and the altar and its furniture from the Chapel being placed in the space at one end. A small platform was placed upon the centre of the floor and covered with a costly Indian carpet and over this was placed the Royal ensign.

Till late at night I was in the Chapel seeing it duly prepared.

Hatfield House, Hertfordshire

Lady Violet Cecil

Daughter-in-law to the Prime Minister, Lord Salisbury. Arthur Balfour had joined his uncle, Lord Salisbury and his cousins for dinner.

They had had a very tiring day, swearing all day.

'*I am quite tired of breaking the Third Commandment*' said Lord Salisbury.

Being men, they could not, of course, give a proper account of all that had happened. We had to cross-examine them minutely and even then they were very unsatisfactory witnesses.

Arthur [Balfour] had travelled up from Osborne with what he called '*the Prince*'. Lord Salisbury, on my other side, corrected him: '*The King*.'

'*He consulted me*,' said Arthur, '*on many points on which I am not very well qualified to advise him and asked me to be early at the Privy Council and so I was*.'

The Council was held in the Levée Room and after the Councillors were assembled, the Duke [of Devonshire] asked the Lord Privy Seal to go and fetch the Prince '*then*,' added Arthur, nodding towards Lord Salisbury, '*he went off and didn't come back for ever so long. What were you doing?*'

'*I went in to see him. He was very much upset. We had a long talk alone. He broke down*' said Lord Salisbury.

'*Well, then they came back and the Prince made a really very good little speech – without notes – very simple, just the speech one would have wished him to make. Only then the Duke moved that it should be made public. And we all agreed, only the Prince had no notes and there was no report, so I am afraid it is just being put together by Stalbridge (brother to the Duke of Westminster) and Rosebery. You'll think it all very jejune. I must tell you*,' said Arthur, turning to Lord Salisbury, '*that your Home Secretary* [Charles Ritchie] *and your President of the Council* [Duke of Devonshire] *have fallen out over the Accession Proclamation. Apparently, there is an old clause about gambling at cards on Sunday which Ritchie wants to keep and Devonshire, for obvious reasons, wants to drop. Indeed, two more notorious breakers of that law than himself and his Sovereign it would be hard to find*.' We laughed. It is a comic position.

By this time Gwenny[17] and I felt that Arthur was getting away from the main subject. '*Well?*' we said. '*Well?*'

17 Lady Gwendolin Cecil, daughter of Lord Salisbury.

'*Well*,' said Arthur, '*then we began to swear and, of course, there were not nearly enough Prayer-books and after we'd sworn as Privy Councillors, we swore allegiance*.'

'*I am sure you did it very badly*,' said Gwenny to her father.

'*Not worse than most*,' said Arthur.

'*The King gave me a nudge not to kneel down. I was rather offended*,' said Lord Salisbury.

'*You knelt down on one knee, I suppose?*' said Gwenny.

'*Oh, we all did that*.'

'*Poor Prince Christian was rather out of it, for the Royalties were always spoken of as the Royal Dukes and he isn't a Royal Duke. He was only made a Privy Councillor so as to have one handy near the Queen to make a quorum. By the way, Arthur, is P—-- a Privy Councillor? I suppose I made him, but I can't remember when.*'

'*Oh, no one but you would have made him*,' said Arthur.

London

George, Duke of Cornwall and York

At 8.30 Papa, Uncle Arthur [Connaught], George [Duke of Cambridge], Christian [Prince Christian of Schleswig-Holstein], Lorne [Duke of Argyll], & the Louis Battenbergs[18] dined with me. After dinner Lord Clarendon (Lord Chamberlain) & Sir Spencer Ponsonby Fane came & we discussed various points connected with the funeral. Bed at 12. Very tired.

---

18 Prince Louis Alexander of Battenberg (1854–1921) and Princess Victoria of Hesse and by Rhine (1863–1950). Granddaughter. Age 37. Eldest daughter of Queen Victoria's third child, Princess Alice, Grand Duchess of Hesse and by Rhine (1843–78), who died of diphtheria in 1878 on the anniversary of the death of her father Prince Albert. During the First World War they changed their name to Mountbatten. Their youngest son, Louis Mountbatten, was to become 1st Earl Mountbatten of Burma. Princess Victoria was grandmother to Prince Philip, Duke of Edinburgh.

Reginald Brett, Viscount Esher

At night, at 10, the King summoned me and Clarendon to discuss the funeral arrangements. All the Royal Dukes were there. A curious gathering to those who remember interviews with the Queen.

The Times

There is one flag in New York which is not lowered in honour of the Queen's memory. It flaunts over the City Hall by order of Mayor Van Wyck. The Mayor explains that he did not even half-mast it for Joubert,[19] though he '*had dined him and honoured him for fighting those who were murdering his people and taking their lands*'. Therefore he will not for the Queen.

The Proclamation:

> We are informed that the Proclamation ceremony will take place at temple Bar at 8.30, which means that at St James's Palace it must be at least half-an-hour earlier. From Temple Bar the heralds' procession will go on to the Royal exchange. No proclamation is to be made either at Charing-cross or at Wood-street.

19 Piet Joubert, the late Commandant-General of the South African Republic. He died from peritonitis after being thrown from his horse during a raid in the Second Boer War at the end of March 1900.

Egypt

Wilfrid Scawen Blunt

Sheykh Obeyd
The Queen is dead and the great Victorian age is at an end.

This is notable news. It will mean great changes in the world, for the long understanding amongst the Emperors that England is not to be quarrelled with during the Queen's lifetime will now give place to freer action.

The Emperor William does not love his uncle, our new king. On the other hand, it may possibly lead to a less bloody regime in South Africa; not that the Prince of Wales very likely is any more humane than his mother, who had a craze for painting the map Imperial red, but because he knows European opinion better and the limitations of England's power and the necessity moderating English arrogance.

The Queen it was easy to flatter and mislead, the only paper she read was the 'Morning Post,' and the People about her did not dare tell her the real truth of things, but the Prince of Wales hears and knows everything that goes on abroad far more than does Lord Salisbury. All this is to the good.

As to Her Majesty personally, one does not like to say all one thinks even in one's journal. By all I have ever heard of her she was in her old age a dignified but rather commonplace good soul, like how many of our dowagers, narrow-minded in her view of things, without taste in art or literature, fond of money, having a certain industry and business capacity in politics, but easily flattered and expecting to be flattered, quite convinced of her own providential position in the world and always ready to do anything to extend and augment it. She has been so long accustomed to success that she seems to have imagined that everything she did was wise and right, and I should not be surprised if the discreditable failure in South Africa had hastened her end.

I see that Roberts went down to Osborne just before the seizure took place, and perhaps she may have insisted upon hearing the whole truth from him and, realising it for the first time, have had the stroke of which she died. We shall probably be kept in the dark about this for a long while, for the public has got to look upon the old lady as a kind of fetish or idol, and nobody, even now she is dead, will dare print a word not to her glorification.

THURSDAY, 24 JANUARY

LONDON

Garter King of Arms

Public proclamation from the gallery at St James's Palace.

We do now hereby, with one voice and consent of tongue and heart, publish and proclaim that the high and mighty prince Albert Edward is now, by the death of our late sovereign of happy memory, become our only lawful and rightful liege lord Edward the Seventh, by the grace of God, king of the United Kingdom of Great Britain and Ireland, Defender of the Faith, Emperor of India. God save the King!

Almeric Fitzroy

Another Council was held at Marlborough House this morning, at which the changes in the Liturgy were approved, and some other Privy Councillors sworn. The Duke of York is to hold the title of Cornwall prefixed to that of York, but not to become Prince of Wales for some time.

The King asked me afterwards to edit the account of the Council for the 'Court Circular.'

He left London immediately for Osborne.

The London Gazette

His Majesty was pleased this Day in Council to declare His Royal Will and Pleasure, That in all the Prayers, Liturgies, and Collects for the Queen, instead of the Word 'Queen,' the Word 'King,' instead of the Word 'Victoria' the Word 'Edward,' instead of the Words 'our Sovereign Lady' the Words 'our Sovereign Lord,' ...

And His Majesty doth strictly charge and command, that no Edition of the Common Prayer be from henceforth printed but with this Amendment; And that in the meantime, till copies of such Edition may be had, all Parsons, Vicars, and Curates within this Realm, do (for the Preventing of Mistakes), with the Pen, correct and amend all such Prayers in their Church.
A. W. Fitzroy.

Egypt

Wilfrid Scawen Blunt

Sheykh Obeyd
The Prince of Wales has been proclaimed as Edward VII and begins his reign with the usual acclamations of the vulgar, the vulgar in this instance including everybody, all his little failings forgotten or hidden well out of sight. He has certain good qualities of amiability and a Philistine tolerance for other people's sins which endear him to rich and poor, from archbishops down to turf book-makers, and the man in the street. He will make an excellent king for twentieth century England.

OSBORNE HOUSE

Sir James Reid

In the morning I was in and out of the Queen's room. Fuchs and Herkomer[20] (who had just arrived to make a sketch) were at work.

Randall Davidson, Bishop of Winchester

I was early at Osborne, seeing to what had been done during the night in fitting up the Chapel.

After breakfast I was again in the Chapel with Princess Beatrice and Princess Christian [Helena], when a message came that the undertaker[21] had arrived. They asked me to see him, as he had no doubt come with the coffin.

Reid had written, on the night the Queen died, particulars about what would be required, and had specially noted that the shell for the Queen's body must be at Osborne on Thursday morning.

I got Sir James Reid and went to the Queen's Room, and the undertaker met us outside the door.

To our surprise he was a rough ordinary man, and we were still more amazed when it practically appeared that, to put it bluntly, the Queen's coffin had been forgotten.

When we asked the man whether he had brought the coffin he said '*No, I have come to take the preliminary measurements.*' We were at a loss what to do, as the man explained that the measurements would have to be sent to London and the making of the shell would then be begun, and that it might be there possibly by the middle or afternoon of the following day but not sooner.

20 Hubert von Herkomer, a Bavarian artist and film maker.

21 William Banting of St James's Street. Royal Undertakers. Having previously conducted the funerals of King George III (1820), George IV (1830), the Duke of Gloucester (1834), the Duke of Wellington (1852), Prince Albert (1861) and Prince Leopold (1884).

We told him this was absolutely out of the question. But he was not a person in authority and could only tell us what had been the orders given him.

Again, I had recourse to the Emperor, and he came and talked over the situation with Reid and myself. We finally arranged that this man from Banting's should be sent in to Cowes to see the leading undertaker there, and that he, instead of Banting, should make the shell immediately and should be pressed to have it ready the same evening. Of course, this was objected to on the part of Banting's man.

Wilhelm II, Emperor of Germany

It is always like this. When an ordinary humble person dies everything is arranged quite easily and with reverence and care. When a 'personage' dies, you fellows all lose your heads and make stupid mistakes which you ought to be ashamed of. The same happens in Germany as in England: You are all alike!

Randall Davidson, Bishop of Winchester

If the occasion had been a less grave and solemn one there would have been much that was humorous in the Emperor's harangue to the rather dull undertaker's assistant.

The Emperor frightened the poor fellow into helpless obedience. The man was simply terrified.

He was so unsuitable a person, as it appeared to me, that we declined to leave him (as he wished) in the room to take the necessary measurements, and as a matter of fact the measurements were taken by the Emperor, Reid, and myself, under the direction of the man, who stood by and told us exactly what he wanted. It was altogether a curious scene.

Sir James Reid

We decided that the shell must be made at once and brought to Osborne by 7.30 tonight, so that the body could be lifted in before dinner. I went to measure the body with the Bantings man, the Kaiser coming with us, and also the Bishop of Winchester whom we met in the passage, and who seemed to think he ought to be there, and who made himself prominent in giving directions.

The Kaiser rather resented this interference and said to me when we came out of the room '*If I were dead and my pastor came in the room like that he would be hauled out by the neck and shot in the Courtyard!*'

At one o'clock I cycled to May Cottage for half an hour to see Susan and Margaret.

Randall Davidson, Bishop of Winchester

A message came from the King in London saying that he wished to have a Celebration of Holy Communion in the Queen's Room as soon as he arrived from London.

The King arrived at 2.30, and at a little before 4 p.m. we had the Service he desired. We had not felt it to be right to move the furniture much in the Queen's Room, and as the room was not large and the furniture was plentiful we had some difficulty in arranging for the large number of Royalties who stated that they desired to take part in the Communion Service. But all was ultimately managed. It was altogether a historic scene.

In the centre lay the little Queen with fresh flowers arranged on the bed, the small Imperial crown lying by the side, her face beginning to lose a little of the fine look it had the previous day, but most calm and peaceful.

I shortened the Service, using special Collect, Epistle, and Gospel, and deliberately did not read the Prayer for the King until after the Gloria and just before the Blessing. This gave, I think, and was felt to give, a significance to the whole.

Sir Frederick Ponsonby

When he [the King] returned a difficult situation arose.

The relations between the two households had always been very cordial so that there was no chance of any unpleasant rows taking place such as were reported to have happened in Germany when first the old Emperor William and later the Emperor Frederick died.

The difficulty we had at Osborne was quite the reverse because everyone behaved so tactfully that whenever a telegram or letter arrived no one would open it.

The Prince of Wales's people hated the idea of taking everything over abruptly, and yet, of course, we had ceased to hold any appointment.

At last Sidney Greville[22] came to me and said that the Prince of Wales had decided that we were all to continue our duties until further orders and go on just as usual with our work, only referring questions to him that required decision.

I was therefore temporarily employed in answering his telegrams, but this did not give me much work. When I heard that Princess Louise was in difficulties I at once offered my help.

This she gladly accepted and I found her trying to deal with two hundred and eighty-one telegrams; after answering hundreds daily this number did not frighten me. I asked her to go through them and dictate answers to those she wished to reply to personally while I took down what she said in shorthand.

She, just like the rest of her family, found no difficulty in expressing herself and dictated some really first-rate answers. The remainder I told her I would answer myself.

22 Sir Sidney Greville, equerry to the Prince of Wales.

Afterwards I heard that she complained of having nothing to do while her sisters remained hard at work.

LONDON

Sir Edward Walter Hamilton

It was settled last night that the Lord Chamberlain was to carry out the funeral arrangements. But the Duke of Norfolk asserted his rights as Earl Marshal and carried the day. The consequence is the Lord Chamberlain is very sorry, and is likely to decline to give assistance. Indeed, it will be lucky if these two ceremonial dignitaries don't come to loggerheads.

Reginald Brett, Viscount Esher

I suggested a 'sea procession.' It would have been a fine thing to have brought the Queen the whole way to London by sea. However, she seems to have given certain directions which are to be followed. No black – no hearse – only a gun-carriage. A military funeral. It is fixed for Saturday, February 2nd, so we have only 10 days in which to make mighty preparations.

Duke of Argyll

She had always had a dislike to the black trappings commonly used, and desired that black should be avoided as far as possible in the hangings and appurtenances used at her funeral, preferring purple and white before these, and even that black horses should be dispensed with. As in the case of the King of Italy, who went to his grave coffined in white and gold only a few short months before in Rome, so was our Queen also to be buried.

The London Gazette

The Earl Marshal's Order for a General Mourning for Her late Most Gracious Majesty Queen Victoria.

IN pursuance of an Order of His Majesty in Council, 24th day of January, 1901, these are to give public notice, that it is expected that all persons upon the present occasion of the death of Her late Majesty of blessed and glorious memory, do put themselves into the deepest Mourning. The said Mourning to begin upon Monday, the 28th day of this instant January.

NORFOLK, Earl Marshal

Lord Chamberlain's Office

January 24, 1901.
ORDERS for the Court, to go into Mourning for Her late Most Gracious Majesty Queen Victoria, of Blessed Memory, viz.: – The Ladies to wear black Dresses, trimmed with Crape, and black Shoes and Gloves, black Fans. Feathers, and Ornaments. The Gentlemen to wear black Court Dress, with black Swords and Buckles. The Mourning to commence from the date of this Order.

The Court to change the Mourning on Wednesday the 24th July next, viz.: – The Ladies to wear black Dresses, with coloured Ribbons, Flowers. Feathers, and Ornaments, or grey or white Dresses, with black Ribbons, Flowers, Feathers, and Ornaments. The Gentlemen to continue the same Mourning. And on Friday the 24th January next, the Court to go out of Mourning.

Princess Marie-Louise of Schleswig-Holstein

(1872–1956) Granddaughter. Age 28. Youngest daughter of Princess Helena.

There was great consternation and bewilderment in the Lord Chamberlain's office, as well as in the Royal Family, as to what was the correct mourning for the Sovereign.

It was sixty-four years since such a tragic event had taken place. No one knew what should be worn; old prints and pictures of long ago were studied to see how to bring up to date and modernize the cumbersome trappings of mourning.

Strange as it may seem, I was appealed to as knowing what was de vignette on such sad occasions abroad. Sixty-four years previously the ladies wore large bonnets rather like coal scuttles; their dresses were trimmed with bombazine; of course, high up to the neck which was swathed in white crêpe.

In order to modernize the coal-scuttle bonnet, I advised that the headdress should be similar to that worn in Germany; namely, a Mary Stuart cap coming to a peak on the forehead, to which was attached at the back a long flowing crêpe veil. This cap and veil, it was decreed, must be worn indoors as well as outside the house. For the trimming of the cashmere dresses, dull crêpe (not the bright crinkly kind) took the place of bombazine. This crêpe had to measure twelve inches in front and twenty inches at the back. Round the neck were folds of white chiffon – décolletage, of course, was not allowed – and deep cuffs of the same material reaching half-way up the elbow. When all the Princesses were assembled together they were really rather imposing, being all dressed alike, and, quite honestly, this mourning uniform was most becoming.

Daily Telegraph

Every woman in the land, be she ever so poor, will want a black gown in order to show her respect for the venerable Queen and it follows that the observance of mourning will affect the lower middle classes more than any other since this article is not always possessed.

Arthur Harding

Born in the Old Nichol, Bethnal Green, in 1886.

It was the most extraordinary thing. Everybody – the children as well – wore black. Everyone was in mourning. Even poor little houses that faced onto the street put a board up and painted it black. All the shops had black shutters up and everyone felt as if they'd lost somebody. It was extraordinary that people who were starving for the best part of their lives should mourn the old Queen.

Kate Frye

I looked out a black coat and skirt of Agnes' to send to Abbie as I know she has not black at all – and of course could not buy any, poor girl – and one would feel it so much now.

Stella [reported that at Whiteleys] the people were standing 8 and 10 deep at the glove counter waiting to be served [with black gloves].

What a blessing we all have a few black garments – it would be a terrible rush to get any made. Last night I took some coloured ribbon from an otherwise all black hat & pinned in a black feather I had by me – so with my black coat and skirt and a black silk front to a blouse I was quite alright.

It seemed a funny sort of day – between a bank holiday and a Sunday.

I never saw such a sight as the shop windows – everything black in them – even the fancy shops and as for the Drapers it looks too awful. Everyone is dressed in mourning – men with the deepest of hat bands etc – not a piece of colour anywhere – and of course black shutters to all the shops. Our future is a blank. All theatres still shut.

The Times

In the great majority of the shops black shutters had been put up or revolving shutters had been partially lowered. In a few instances black drapery was in process of hanging over the windows. In many of the clubs the blinds were drawn; the flags on omnibuses were lowered, and the cabmen and omnibus drivers almost to a man had fastened a piece of crape on their whips. The Courts naturally met, only immediately to rise. As was befitting in the very heart of the Empire, signs of mourning were everywhere. Some emblem of mourning was worn by practically everybody. The Stock Exchange was closed. At Windsor Castle the Royal Standard drooped half-mast high on the Round Tower. Funeral braids are displayed at the shops, some being draped in black and violet material, and portraits of the late Queen are displayed in many of the shop windows.

To the Editor of The Times

Sir,

Apropos of the order for the Court to go into mourning for her late Most Gracious Majesty Queen Victoria for 12 months, may I be permitted to point out, as representing the retail drapery trade, that coloured fabrics, ribbons, &c., are ordered from the manufacturer three or four months in advance; in fact, the goods ordered in October and November last are now being delivered.

As the Court will keep in mourning for the period above stated, the example will naturally be followed by the loyal subjects of his Most Gracious Majesty the King, with the result that manufacturers and wholesale and retail establishments will suffer enormous loss on goods actually manufactured, for the reason that before the dawn of January 1902, these coloured fabrics will have depreciated in value and, probably, also be out of fashion.

I know that his Most Gracious Majesty the King appreciates the nation's heartfelt desire to mourn with him. I know, too, that his Majesty would not wittingly cause sorrow or trouble to any of his subjects, but this I fear must inevitably be the case, unless an order is issued by the Earl Marshal fixing the limit for public mourning.

Traders having already suffered by reason of the war, I venture most humbly to suggest that three months' public mourning would meet the wishes of the people, and such an order would tend to greatly stimulate trade.

I am, Sir, yours obediently,

JOS. R. QUILTER, Secretary.

Drapers' Chamber of Trade, 28, New Bridge-street, E.C.

Osborne House

Sir James Reid

I had a talk with Mrs Tuck who, the night before, had read me the Queen's instructions about what the Queen had ordered her to put in the coffin, some of which none of the family were to see, and as she could not carry out Her Majesty's wishes without my help, she asked me to cooperate.

Later I helped her and the nurse to put a satin dressing gown and garter ribbon and star, etc., on the Queen. We cut off her hair and rearranged the flowers.

I was very busy in the evening and could not get out, so Susan came up and saw me for a few minutes.

The shell came up too late for the body to be put in till tomorrow. I saw the King repeatedly about this and other matters. The Queen begged me for the body to be left till the morning – 'no smell'.

Randall Davidson, Bishop of Winchester

After Dinner, at 10 p.m., the King desired to receive formally the members of the late Queen's Household.

We were accordingly marshalled outside the Council Room and entered successively, the King saying a few words to each as we took our places. Nothing could have been simpler or more dignified than his action, though perhaps the proceedings were a little over-formal, and it was strange for the men who had arranged everything in the house for years – Bigge, Edwards, etc – to find themselves introduced by a new Equerry into the Sovereign's presence.

Sir James Reid

After dinner we were all received by the King and kissed hands.

After this I went to meet the Queen's shell and superintended its being carried into her room and being placed by the bed, on the other side from where she was lying.

The bluejackets, under Lieutenant Pelly of the Victoria and Albert, having come up to carry the coffin downstairs were kept waiting all evening, and then were allowed to file past the body and were sent back with orders to return at ten tomorrow morning.

The Duke of York came back from Marlborough House ailing – feverish – cough – and lumber pain. I sent him to bed.

Act IV

Chaos & Confusion

25–31 January 1901

Friday, 25 January

Osborne House

Randall Davidson, Bishop of Winchester

I had a broken and disturbed night, and had to start very early next morning for London.

I left Cowes by the steamer at 7 a.m. to be present at Ryle's[1] consecration to Exeter in Westminster Abbey. The whole scene was in strange contrast to the surroundings in which I had been plunged for a few days.

Lady Susan Reid

All is rather in a state of chaos here at present and everyone still fearfully busy. Jamie is the mainstay at the house! and is wanted and consulted by all, and has everything to arrange and settle.

Jamie has to carry out all her last wishes as to what she wears, and photographs of the Prince Consort and her children are to be put in, also a garment worked by Princess Alice.[2] She is to be in a white silk robe and the Order of the Garter on. I fear it will be a very sad moment for our Jamie to feel that after that, there will be nothing more he can do for Her.

These last days he has not left the house, except for a few minutes, as he felt she was still his charge. She wished to have no lying in State and therefore embalming was not necessary, and she is to have a Military Funeral as Head of the Army. She left very minute

1 Herbert Edward Ryle, appointed Bishop of Exeter in December 1900.

2 Princess Alice, Grand Duchess of Hesse and by Rhine (1843–78). The first of Queen Victoria's children to die.

directions as to all she wants done, which is a comfort, as it saves all discussions!

Sir James Reid

At nine I saw the Duke of York in bed with a feverish attack.[3]

At 9.30 I went to the Queen's room, and arranged with Mrs Tuck and Miss Stewart[4] to put on the floor of the Queen's coffin over the layer of charcoal 1½ inches thick the various things (dressing gown of Prince Consort, cloak of his own embroidered by Princess Alice, the Prince Consort's plaster hand, numerous photographs, etc.) which Her Majesty had left instructions with them to put in. Over these was laid the quilted cushion made to fit the shape of the coffin, so that it looked as if nothing had been put in.

I then got Woodford and his men to move the shell round to the side of the Queen and on the same level as the bed on which she was lying. I sent them out into the adjoining dressing room.

The Princess of Wales came, and she and the King remained a few minutes alone in the room, and the Queen laid some flowers on the body. Then I brought in the Emperor of Germany (the Queen having gone out), the Duke of Connaught, Prince Arthur of Connaught,[5] Mrs Tuck, Misses Stewart and Ticking,[6] Woodford, Scott and Spenser. We lifted the Queen into the coffin, Mrs Tuck and I taking the head, Misses Stewart and Ticking the feet, the King and Duke of Connaught, the Emperor and Prince Arthur the straps (laid under the body) on the left, over the coffin, and Woodford, Scott and Spenser, on the bed on the right side of the body.

Then all the Royalties went out, leaving Mrs Tuck, Misses Stewart and Ticking with me, and they rearranged the Queen's dressing gown, the veil and the lace. Then I packed the sides with

3 This developed into German measles and he was unable to attend the funeral.

4 Miss Stewart, dresser to the Queen.

5 Prince Arthur of Connaught (1883–1938). Grandson. Age 18.

6 Miss Ticking, dresser to the Queen.

bags of charcoal in muslin and put in the Queen's left hand the photo of Brown and his hair in a case (according to her private instructions), which I wrapped in tissue paper, and covered with Queen Alexandra's flowers.

After all was done I asked White, Shooter, Brown and Gordon who were nearby to come and see the Queen and then went to the drawing room and asked the Royal ladies there to come and have a last look. They all came, the Princess of Wales, the Duchess of Coburg[7] and her daughter Beatrice,[8] the Duchess of Connaught, and her two daughters,[9] the Duchess of Albany,[10] and her daughter,[11] the Duchess of York, the Princesses Christian and Thora, Princess Beatrice, Princess Louise, and Princess Ena.[12]

When they went out I asked the King to let Miss Phipps come, which she did, with Miss Knollys. Then I got from him leave for Clinton, Edwards, Bigge, M'Neill, Carington[13] and Fritz [Ponsonby] to come and look, which they did. The King sent for the Munshi[14] to come.

Then all went out and in the presence of the King, the Emperor, the Duke of Connaught, Prince Arthur, the Duke of Coburg[15] and

---

7 Princess Maria, Dowager Duchess of Saxe-Coburg and Gotha (1853–1920). Daughter-in-law. Age 47.

8 Princess Beatrice of Saxe-Coburg and Gotha (1884–1966). Granddaughter. Age 16.

9 Princess Margaret of Connaught, *Daisy* (1822–1920). Granddaughter. Age 18. Princess Patricia of Connaught, *Patsy* (1886–1974). Granddaughter. Age 14.

10 Princess Helena, Dowager Duchess of Albany (1861–1922). Daughter-in-law. Age 39. Widow of Prince Leopold, Duke of Albany (1853–84), the Queen's youngest son who had haemophilia and had died in 1884.

11 Princess Alice of Albany (1883–1981). Granddaughter. Age 17.

12 Princess Victoria of Battenberg, *Ena* (1887–1969). Youngest grandchild. Age 12. Only daughter of Princess Beatrice. Later to marry King Alfonso XIII of Spain.

13 William Carrington, Liberal MP, equerry to the Queen and Master of the Buckhounds.

14 Abdul Karim, known as 'the Munshi'. Indian secretary to Queen Victoria for her last fifteen years and generally disliked by the Royal Household.

15 Prince Charles, Duke of Saxe-Coburg and Gotha, Duke of Albany (1884–1954). Grandson. Age 16. Son of Prince Leopold. Prince Charles was born after his father's death.

myself, Woodford and his two men came in and screwed down the lid, and carried the coffin, covered with a white pall, into the passage at the top of the stairs, whence a party of bluejackets from the yacht carried it downstairs into the dining room which had been prepared as Chapelle Ardente, where soldiers now mounted guard, and my duties were over with the Queen after twenty years' service!

Sir Frederick Ponsonby

The 60th Rifles had been sent for from Parkhurst Barracks to provide the guard over the coffin, but when they arrived and asked for orders no one quite knew what the procedure was. The men had never been taught to reverse arms and the drill book was dumb on the subject. I was appealed to under the misapprehension that I had done this sort of thing before, but I was really very hazy about the subject.

A most intelligent and smart captain, however, after consultation with Sir John M'Neill[16] and myself, evolved a ceremonial for relieving the men every hour, as the strong perfume of the flowers seemed to upset them at first, and it was arranged that four men should stand with reversed arms at the four corners while one of the Household should keep watch at the foot of the coffin.

The Duke of Connaught, however, found out that it was the privilege of the Queen's Company, Grenadier Guards, to mount guard over the defunct Sovereign, and a telegram was sent off summoning them at once.

They arrived with two officers, St John Coventry and Myles Ponsonby.[17] Coventry was extremely sketchy about the whole thing and simply copied the 60th Rifles. When however, Arthur Lloyd, the Captain of the Queen's Company, Grenadier Guards, came along it

16 Major-General Sir John Carstairs M'Neill VC. Equerry to the Queen.

17 Myles Ponsonby, a distant relation of Frederick Ponsonby, descended from the 3rd Earl of Bessborough.

was a very different thing and the changing of the sentries became a most impressive sight all done in slow time. In addition to the Grenadiers one member of the late Queen's Household kept watch. I found this very trying, not only on account of the very strong scent of the tuberoses and gardenias, but because I could ill afford the time.

The dining-room was hung round with curtains and draperies. The room was lighted by eight huge candles and there were palms round the room in addition to masses of wreaths. It was all gorgeous with colour and most impressive.

George, Duke of Cornwall and York

Had a fair night & feel better, temperature still 100 so Reid would not let me get up.

At 10.45 darling Grandmama was put in her coffin & carried down by bluejackets of the Royal Yacht to the dining room where the coffin was placed.

May sat with me part of the day & Sir James Reid came to see me several times.

Mary, Duchess of Cornwall and York

We are to be called Duke & Duchess of Cornwall & York and I don't think the King intends to create George Prince of Wales.

To Aunt Augusta:[18]

The Queen looked so beautiful after death, like a marble statue, & much younger. Now she lies in her coffin in the dining room which is beautifully arranged as a chapel, the coffin is covered

---

18 Princess Augusta, Dowager Grand Duchess of Mecklenberg-Strelitz (1822–1916). Granddaughter of George III and cousin to Queen Victoria. Age 78. Present at the coronation of William IV, age 9, and at his funeral, age 15. Her brother George was Duke of Cambridge.

with the coronation robes & her little diamond crown & the garter lie on a cushion above her head – 4 huge Grenadiers watch there day and night, it is so impressive & fine, yet so simple. You would howl if you could see it all – We go from time to time & the feeling of peace in that room is most soothing to one's feelings.

I believe this is the first time that the Heir Apparent has not been created Prince of Wales! I dislike departing from tradition. [Princess Mary enclosed some pressed flowers taken from the Queen's bedroom.]

Augusta, Dowager Grand Duchess of Mecklenberg-Strelitz

To Princess May

Need I say, I wept over those flowers that had layed by Her side? But, when my tears were dried my ire was up & hot that the legitimate historical Title is not to be continued nor borne by you & George! Oh! what a terrible mistake so to upset old traditions! and why? because he will not be superseded? what can it be else? What reason can the King give?

LONDON

New York Times

King Edward, escorted by a squadron of the Horse Guards and accompanied by the Duke of Cornwall and York, Prince Christian of Schleswig-Holstein, the Duke of Saxe-Coburg and Gotha, and others, left Marlborough House at 11 o'clock to take the train for Osborne. The crowds thronged the streets through which his Majesty passed, and the great cheering was in strong contrast with the silence which greeted his arrival in London.

The vagaries of an apparently harmless lunatic occasioned some excitement at Victoria Station.

While the King was entering the train, a well-dressed individual bearing a letter addressed to his Majesty was permitted to pass the barriers. He hurried to an equerry and said he wished to present the letter to the King personally. The man was handed over to the police. The envelope contained a telegraph form, on which were the words: '*I wish to see my beloved Queen.*'

Almeric Fitzroy

I hear that a heated discussion took place yesterday as to the persons who should be charged with the responsibility of the Queen's funeral.

There is some direction that all matters connected with the funeral of the King, Queen, or Heir Apparent were vested in the Lord Chamberlain.

The Duke of Norfolk maintained, however, that his right to bury the Sovereign, as Earl Marshal of England, should not suffer any derogation.

It required some courage on the part of the Duke to overcome his natural modesty, at a time when the Press had been inflaming the public mind against him for his so-called indiscretion[19] in Rome; but in the next ten days he may have cause to repent having so strenuously preferred his claim, as without any regular organisation he will have to arrange all the details of a notable pageant I am afraid, with no great help from the Lord Chamberlain's officials.

19 Henry Fitzalan-Howard, 15th Duke of Norfolk, the premier peer of the United Kingdom and a leading Roman Catholic had travelled to Rome on a pilgrimage and prayed for the restoration of temporal power to the Pope, causing an uproar in the British press.

Sir Edward Walter Hamilton

At the request of the Duke of Norfolk, I went to the temporary offices of the Earl Marshal this morning to attend the first meeting of the Committee for carrying out the funeral arrangements.

The London procession will not be very easy to manage. It is I believe wholly out of order to have carriages in the procession of a military funeral; and yet everybody won't be able to ride. So riding and walking will have to be combined; and it is not easy to get the big horses to walk slow enough.

Almeric Fitzroy

This afternoon the leaders in both Houses of Parliament addressed themselves to the delivery of their panegyrics on the late Queen.

Mary Monkswell

I went down to the House of Lords for the Vote of Condolence. There was a great crowd. There were more peers & Privy Councillors present than I have ever seen, & such a terrible crowd of ladies that I had a most uncomfortable 20 minutes standing in the very narrow passage for the doors of the Peeresses Gallery to be unlocked.

The scene was most impressive, the crowds of peers & all the ladies in mourning, indeed the scene & feeling were more impressive than the speeches.

Lord Salisbury [Prime Minister] spoke first, his voice was quite shaky, when he began, and I thought he purposely avoided too moving an address for fear he himself should break down. Then Lord Kimberley [Leader of the Liberal opposition] spoke, not very well. The best speech was undoubtedly that of the old Archbishop of Canterbury, Dr. Temple.[20] He is a stiff old tutor of Balliol not given to raising emotion, & in his 80th year. He seemed almost over-powered when he began, but pulled himself together & spoke out in his harsh voice – that was the first time when I felt the electric thrill run through me, I was glad not to be severely thrilled, for the occasion itself was so great & sad that it was as much as one could bear. The old Duke of Cambridge, who is older than the Queen, sat on the cross benches. Next to him sat Earl Roberts, such a little shrunk brown man. It was so strange to see all these beautiful peeresses & blooming girls in their magnificent mourning, they looked of course extraordinarily handsome.

Almeric Fitzroy

The greatest triumph, however, was achieved in the House of Commons by Mr. Balfour. In exquisite sentences of moving and measured eloquence he depicted the laborious life in which the Queen had spent herself for the nation's service, and brought the image of her daily toil most vividly before his hearers by a pathetic reference to the last wavering signature and the pile of documents untouched by the vanished hand.

On leaving the House I was attacked by Lord Acton[21] for having allowed the King to commit the 'howler' of describing the last two Edwards as his ancestors. He appeared to think he had completely established his case by quoting the well-known story of Lord Macaulay's[22] correction of the Queen when she called James II her

20 Frederick Temple, Archbishop of Canterbury (1896–1902). He was succeeded by Randall Davidson, Bishop of Winchester.

21 John Dalberg-Acton, 1st Baron Acton. Historian and Liberal statesman who became the first editor of *The Cambridge Modern History*.

22 Thomas Macaulay, 1st Baron Macaulay (1800–59). Historian and Whig politician and author of *The History of England from the Accession of James the Second*.

ancestor, so slow is the tradition of Lord Macaulay's infallibility to disappear. I was not much impressed, and was glad to find my view supported by the most authoritative of modern dictionaries, wherein 'ancestor' is explained as '*one, whether a progenitor or a collateral relative, who has preceded another in the course of inheritancwe*.' I told Arthur Balfour afterwards of the find, who charged me to rub it into Acton, which I did, without, however, eliciting any withdrawal of his opprobrious language!

Saturday, 26 January

Osborne House

Randall Davidson, Bishop of Winchester

I crossed by early boat and got back to Osborne by 9.30. The coffin had during the night been moved down to the Chapel, and we had a little Service there at 10.15, most of the Royal Family being present.

The Times

The Lord Chamberlain is authorised to announce that any ladies or gentlemen of Queen Victoria's Household who may wish to visit Osborne to see the chapelle ardente are, by the King's command, permitted to do so up to Wednesday next inclusive.

Some forty journalists and artists filed in from the quiet surroundings of Osborne.

For a moment they stood in a yellow drawing-room, looking out on to the terrace, and over the sea; and then, turning to the right, they were in so much of the dining-room as has been appropriated to the uses of a chapelle ardente.

The sight was wonderful, awe-inspiring, and yet, in its way, comforting both as a whole and in detail. Blackness and gloom there were none, for there was the light of day through the opened folding doors, and the silver candelabras were burning.

Of black drapery, of black at all, indeed, there was none, save here and there a ribbon attached to a wreath, and except in the dress of the few who filed silently and sadly round the coffin.

The small portion of the dining-room used for the sacred purpose was parted from the rest by a red hanging, from top to bottom of which hung a huge Union Jack.

Scarlet were the four tall Grenadiers, who stood at the four corners of the coffin, with their backs towards it, with their bodies bent in statuesque stillness over the butts of their inverted rifles. They seemed scarcely to breathe; one hardly realised that they were alive; and the posture was one of unspeakable and helpless grief.

Then, after the first moment of blank bewilderment the eye began to take in the object of grand and central interest – the coffin containing all that was mortal of England's greatest and best Queen.

There, in the casket of cedar and lead and oak, lay the heart of England, and many of England's hopes, not dead, but ready to rise again.

On the coffin, placed by the King's hand, was the diamond crown, there, too, were the jewel and ribbon of the Garter; and about the coffin was draped the ermine robe of the Garter.

Under the coffin was the Royal Standard, with part of the Scottish Lion showing at one corner, and part of the Irish Harp at another, and below that, and extending beyond it, a rich Indian shawl.

At the foot of the coffin and around it were wreaths of laurel, of lilies, of bays, and of scarlet azaleas, placed on the floor, was a colossal crown of foliage and purest blue flowers.

So, half-reluctantly, by reason of the quiet beauty of the little scene; half-willingly, because the solemnity was almost oppressive, one left the room and passed to the open air.

For the present, seeing that the interval before the funeral is still long, it will be convenient to state, by official request, that it is asked that wreaths intended for the funeral of the February 2 should be addressed to the Master of the Household at Windsor Castle.

George, Duke of Cambridge

I got a summons to go to Osborne to-day. Left Victoria at 3.50, Dolly Teck[23] going with me, instead of my Equerry, for whom there was no room. On reaching Dockyard Station Admiral Hotham strongly urged me not to attempt to go over to Cowes as it was blowing and raining so hard, and embarking and landing being consequently so slippery and difficult, but to stay at the Admiralty House with him for the night, as no Royal Yacht had come over for me; so I decided to do so, and was most comfortably put up for the night.

Lord Edward Pelham-Clinton

I am at home the whole day, busy answering telegrams and writing. Have a business interview with the King. Princess Victoria and Prince and Princess Charles of Denmark arrive 3.15. Duke of Cambridge[?], Duke of Teck, Duke of Norfolk, Earl Roberts and Mr Brodrick [Secretary of State for War] arrive late.

Household dinner 23. Royal dinner of 22.

23 Prince Adolphus, Duke of Teck, younger brother of Mary, Duchess of Cornwall and York. Known as Dolly, he relinquished his German titles in 1917 to become Marquess of Cambridge. George, Duke of Cambridge was his uncle.

Sunday, 27 January

Osborne House

Randall Davidson, Bishop of Winchester

Went to Whippingham for early Service and breakfasted at the Rectory. Morning Service at 12 was rather of a special character attended by the King & Queen, Emperor of Germany and some twenty other Royalties besides a very full congregation of Whippingham people and of course all the Royal Household also Lord Roberts. I preached.

George, Duke of Cambridge

Breakfasted at 9.30, and then I started for Osborne at 10.30, the Alberta Royal Yacht having come over to fetch me. Got in at 12.15, being put up at Osborne Lodge very comfortably in ground floor rooms.

Drove up to the House for lunch at 1.45, and saw the whole family there assembled. It was a very sad meeting.

The Times

The GERMAN EMPEROR, on the occasion of the anniversary of his [42nd] birthday, has been appointed by the King, a Field-Marshal in the British Army.

George, Duke of Cambridge

The Emperor and Crown Prince,[24] a nice tall lad had gone on board his yacht, the Hohenzollern, and the King and all the Princes here, with the exception of myself, went to visit him and congratulate him on his birthday there, but I could not attempt it, as the gale was so heavy.

Randall Davidson, Bishop of Winchester

I spent the afternoon at Osborne, having a great deal of talk to the Duke of Norfolk, who had come as Earl Marshal to arrange about the Funeral Processions, &c.

He was curiously ignorant of many of the things that everybody else knew. Naturally he did not even try to settle anything about the Services, but he might at least have got up the topography of Windsor.

He had no idea how far it was from the Great Western Station to St. George's Chapel, and when I pointed out to him that his procession as arranged would be far past St. George's Chapel before the coffin left the Station, and therefore could not move at all, he was nonplussed.

It was at my suggestion (though no doubt others would have made it later) that the route was altered to go along Park Street and up the Hill to the Castle.

He had been much interested and puzzled at seeing lying on the coffin the little crucifix before referred to. It appeared to be new to him to learn that the Lutherans (and therefore the Prince Consort) had no objections to a crucifix, and that the Queen had never shared the antipathy of English Protestants to that figure.

24 Wilhelm, Crown Prince of Germany (1882–1951). Great-grandson. Age 18.

George, Duke of Cambridge

Called on the Duke of York, who has got a chill and is ill in bed. Returned to the Cottage till dinner time, paying the Emperor my birthday visit before dinner. All the Royalties dined together and soon broke up.

Randall Davidson, Bishop of Winchester

After dinner I had more talk with the Duke of Norfolk and others about the Funeral arrangements.

I also had a very long conversation with Lord Roberts, who was most interesting, about the schemes for war memorials in South Africa, and especially the plan for the Cathedral at Capetown. He warmly endorses it, and, had the Queen lived, I cannot doubt that his recommendation would have led her to throw her weight into it as he desires. What may now happen who can say?

Lord Edward Pelham-Clinton

Blowing a gale. The German Emperor's birthday. The whole Royal Family go to Church at Whippingham, the Bishop of Winchester preaches. I am unable to go being very busy. At home all day. The King goes on board the Emperor's yacht to offer congratulations.

Royal dinner 25. Household dinner of 22.

Monday, 28 January

Osborne House

Randall Davidson, Bishop of Winchester

The King held an Investiture of the Garter for the Crown Prince of Germany. He did it with great dignity and even pomp, so far as pomp was possible in the circumstances.

All the officers in the house were in full uniform. I had to appear as Prelate (not in the robe, which of course was not with me, but in evening dress, with ribbon, etc.), and the King marshalled us round the room, invited all the German officers from the Hohernzollern, and made a speech to the Crown Prince before investing him.

The whole thing was very well done and created evidently a marked impression upon the Germans.

It was a curious accident that so many K.G's were in the House and able to appear.

George, Duke of Cambridge

Drove up to lunch at the House, after first attending a Chapter of the Order of the Garter.

The King made a very fine and noble address to the young Prince, in which he referred to the Emperor's presence, and the affectionate relationship existing between the two families.

Baron Eckardstein

To Baron Holstein

The most cordial relations conceivable prevail, not only between the Kaiser and the King, but also with the Queen[25] and other members of the Royal Family.

At the investiture of the Crown Prince with the Garter to-day, the King made an address in the most moving language; referring to the close family ties between himself and the House of Hohenzollern, and ended by pointing out that the Kaiser by hastening to the bedside of the Queen, and by staying in England until the funeral, had aroused a profound and permanent sentiment of gratitude and respect, not only in the family circle but throughout the whole British race.

The Kaiser told me that he had had long political conversations with the King and that they were both of the same opinion. The King had a strong dislike, both for Russia and France and had expressed himself in correspondingly strong language about them. When the Kaiser called the King's attention to the symptoms of a rapprochement between the United States and Russia, King Edward became very grave and said he looked on such a coalition as a great danger for the whole of Europe.

Lord Lansdowne[26] had referred to the old doctrine of the Balance of Power between the European States treating it as still being in the hands of England. To this the Kaiser had replied that the Balance of Power rested at present with the twenty-two German Army Corps; adding that England was no longer in a position to keep apart from the rest of Europe but must combine with the Continent.

25 The relationship between Queen Alexandra's Danish Royal Family and the German Royal Family of the Kaiser had been severely strained since the Prussian annexation of the Danish province of Schleswig-Holstein in 1864.

26 Henry Petty-Fitzmaurice, 5th Marquess of Lansdowne. Foreign Secretary.

The Kaiser had throughout made no mention of Germany but referred always to the Continent as a whole.

King Edward expressed himself very strongly as to the attitude of the English Roman Catholic clergy, who had refused to hold memorial services on the day of the Queen's funeral because she had not belonged to the one true Church.

He also spoke with resentment of the behaviour of Prince Ferdinand of Bulgaria.[27] The Prince had offered to come over for the funeral ceremony; but had made it a condition that he should be better treated than at the last Jubilee, when he had not been given proper precedence. After an exchange of telegrams, the Prince had said that he regretted he could not come to London, as he inferred from the British Government's communication that he would not be given the precedence to which he was entitled.
ECKARDSTEIN.

Baron Holstein

To Baron Eckardstein

Berlin

DEAR ECKARDSTEIN,
I sent on your interesting report through the usual channels.

As to Bulgaria, Ferdinand's howl of rage at being warned off London had already reached us from Sofia. I doubt whether people in England, where the Battenberg legend is still cultivated, have any lively affection for the Prince's personality.

It is very reassuring from the point of view of the Kaiser's personal safety that it looks as though he would not stay in London.

27 Elected as Prince Ferdinand I of Bulgaria in 1886, Queen Victoria described him as '... totally unfit ... delicate, eccentric and effeminate ... should be stopped at once'. His father, Prince August of Saxe-Coburg and Gotha, was first cousin to the Queen.

The dangers of such a stay are so obvious that I suppose either the Royal Family or the Government will have found some reason or other against it.

If the Royalties at Osborne are really reconciled again we can only rejoice; but matters would have a different aspect if it occurred to Salisbury for example, to exploit the candour and compliance of His Majesty in order to secure some binding promise.

It is your business, dear friend, to watch carefully for every indication of this in London official circles in order that proper precautions may be taken in time.

I can scarcely suppose that such an attempt will be made by the Royal Family but what the British Ministers may be concocting, if we can't see – you probably can.

See that you don't catch cold at the funeral.

Yours sincerely,

HOLSTEIN

Randall Davidson, Bishop of Winchester

I had rather a worrying day with a great deal of waiting for interviews with the King, which he wished for in connexion with the Funeral details. My final interview was not till 11 p.m.

There was some anxiety all day owing to the illness of the Duke of York, which had become rather serious, and Sir Francis Laking was evidently nervous.

Throughout the afternoon I was closeted with Edwards, Bigge, and Ponsonby successively, discussing their own future plans.

At night I finally settled with the King the details of what part should be taken by each of the Clergy in the Funeral Services at Windsor.

Strange to say he had with his usual interest in the personal details of ceremonial discussed this with me on the very evening of the Queen's death, on the staircase at Osborne, not more than an hour after she died. I have retained the pencil memorandum made with him at that moment.

I did not get home to Edwards's house till midnight. E.M.D. [Edith, his wife] had been hard at work there all the afternoon over my letters.

Lord Edward Pelham-Clinton

Cold and very heavy rain at times. Duke and Duchess of Connaught go to London for the night. At 10 a.m. an Investiture of the Garter of Crown Prince of Germany – all in Levée dress, the whole Royal Family and their Suites present, with Duke of Norfolk, Earl Roberts, Bishop of Winchester as Prelate of the Order of the Garter.

Royal dinner of 22. Household-20.

Tuesday, 29 January

Osborne House

Randall Davidson, Bishop of Winchester

I was early at Osborne, and after breakfast the King sent for me about the Archbishop's Privy Council Service to be used throughout the Kingdom on the day of the funeral. We had some difficulty in understanding exactly what the Archbishop intended, and after I had sent him a telegram conveying the King's approval of the Services, we had to send a special messenger to Lambeth about some apparent misprints.

[Cosmo] Lang of Portsea came to pay a visit to the Chapel and lunched at Osborne. I had some talk with him, and arranged, with the King's approval, for his taking a short Memorial Service on board the Yacht at Portsmouth on Saturday morning before the departure for Windsor.

Cosmo Lang, Vicar of Portsea

I went over from Portsea; and on arrival at Osborne was taken to the chapel.

The first and most arresting impression was the stillness and silence of the Guardsmen standing around with bent heads and muskets reversed. They seemed scarcely alive – rather statues embodying the grief of the people.

Fortunately, there was no one else in the chapel, so I was able to have some minutes of quiet thought and prayer, realising all that the passing of the great Queen meant.

I lunched with the Household; and had some talk with the Bishop of Winchester afterwards about the service which was proposed for the funeral.

While we were talking in the corridor outside the Household dining-room, a small neat figure, quietly dressed came up. I thought it was somebody's servant: but I noticed that the Bishop turned round and bowed. Then I saw the upturned ends of the moustache and realised that it was the German Emperor. He asked if he could be of any service: said that his one wish there was to be serviceable and to show his love for his grandmother and then, after some more talk, he went out for a quiet walk in the garden. I have heard since how extraordinarily tactful he was.

Randall Davidson, Bishop of Winchester

E.M.D. and I walked with Lang to Cowes, and we called on Launcelot Smith, whom I had not seen since I parted from him early on the Sunday morning nine days before.

On that occasion he lent me, at my request, his little battered, torn copy of Walsham How's 'Pastorin Parochia'! This book I used throughout all the ministry both to the Queen and to the mourners, etc, afterwards. It has thus become rather historic.

I promised that Launcelot Smith should have it back with an inscription recording what use it had been put to, and his pleasure is great in possessing it.

I dined at Osborne, and saw the Princesses at night quietly.

Sir Frederick Ponsonby

King Edward sent for me and told me he wished me to take charge of all the funeral arrangements at Windsor. He impressed on me that the service at St. George's Chapel would be arranged with the Dean[28] by the Lord Chamberlain, and that I would have nothing to do with that. All I had to do was to arrange the procession and give orders to the troops, police, etc., at Windsor.

I am not sure that it was a wise thing to put someone in charge of the Windsor part of the funeral who would have to take part in the funeral *cortege* starting from Osborne.

Lord Edward Pelham-Clinton

Fine but cold. The Mistress of the Robes[29] and several Queen's Ladies come at luncheon time to see the Chapelle Ardente. A very short walk at 4.30 the first for a week! The Duke of York has German Measles in the house.

Royal Dinner of 22. Household dinner of 20.

28 The Very Reverend Philip Eliot, Dean of Windsor, 1891–1917.

29 Lady Louisa Hamilton, Duchess of Buccleuch and Queensberry.

LONDON

Lord Gower

I went to Kensington. I found my nephew[30] by himself. Nothing can be conceived more melancholy than London now appears, clubs, etc., with their blinds drawn down, and Kensington Palace was naturally in the deepest mourning. Lorne has felt very deeply the death of the Queen, who was quite like a mother to him. For thirty years, he said, he had received nothing but kindness from the Queen, and not one word of anything but affection. Mr Spottiswoode, the publisher, called to see L. about the life of the Queen which Lorne is going to write.

WEDNESDAY, 30 JANUARY

WINDSOR

Sir Frederick Ponsonby

I decided to go to Windsor by the earliest train, and telegraphed to the Mayor, the head of the police, and the Officer Commanding the troops, to meet me.

When I arrived at Windsor I went to the Town Hall and discussed all the arrangements with the Mayor. He called in the police officials and everything went well. The officer commanding the troops was luckily David Kinloch,[31] a most capable and first-rate organizer, and I went over all the ground with him.

We decided that in view of the fact that there would be colossal crowds the procession, instead of going straight from the station to St. George's Chapel, should go down High Street, Park

30 John Campbell, 9th Duke of Argyll, better known as Lorne, derived from the courtesy title, Marquess of Lorne, which he used until 1900.

31 Lieutenant-Colonel Sir David Kinloch of Gilmerton, 1st Battalion, Grenadier Guards.

Street, and then up to the Castle through the gates at the bottom of the Long Walk. I told him that the funeral procession itself was being managed by the Earl Marshal and that, beyond having a few officers available to marshal the procession, he need not trouble about that. As everything seemed satisfactorily arranged I returned to Osborne in the evening.

LONDON

Sir Edward Walter Hamilton

I went to see Francis Knollys this morning at Marlborough House. The King is indeed lucky to have such a man at his beck and call. He could not have anyone with better judgment and greater tact.

The King was apparently quite satisfied with the result of his talk with Beach[32] yesterday, and so was Beach himself. The King thought Beach quite reasonable, and Beach thought the King quite reasonable because there was no hint given at the necessity of a larger Civil List, except as regards provision for the three Princesses.[33]

It is premature at present to say whether the provision made for Queen Victoria in 1837 is adequate now. What has to be ascertained is how do the expenses which the King will be obliged and expected to incur now compare with those of the Queen 63 years ago.

There is no doubt there have been great abuses in the Royal Household – waste and extravagance; but even allowing for that I expect it will be necessary to raise the Civil List – the present King is believed to have been saddled with both Osborne and

32 Sir Michael Hicks Beach, Chancellor of the Exchequer.

33 King Edward VII's three daughters. Princess Louise, Duchess of Fife (1867–1931). Granddaughter. Age 33. Princess Victoria of Wales (1868–1935). Granddaughter. Age 32. Maud, Princess Carl of Denmark (1869–1938). Granddaughter. Age 31.

Balmoral, and he has besides Sandringham which he would never give up.

If an increase is inevitable, it may be better to make the increase as little *apparent* as possible by relieving the Civil List of some of its present charges. Beach wants me to go into the matter along with Spring Rice (Auditor of the Civil List) and Esher, and if possible to get hold of someone to represent the Civil List.

Osborne House

Randall Davidson, Bishop of Winchester

Wednesday was a quieter day, as most of the arrangements had now been made.

E.M.D. and I had a long walk by the sea in Osborne grounds. Parratt, who had arrived from Windsor with some men and boys from St George's Choir, helped us with a service in the little Chapel. The choir sang Anthems and Hymns most beautifully. The whole Royal Family were present and appreciated it greatly.

Then came a curious episode.

It had been arranged, by the Princesses' request, that one of the Anthems in the great Funeral Service in St George's should be the Russian Anthem from the Office for the Faithful departed.

I felt it my duty to point out to the King that the use of this Anthem on such an occasion would certainly hurt the feelings of very many and might do real harm. I had some difficulty in getting an interview with him about it, but the moment I explained the matter he saw it and felt that it must be altered, but that his sisters would make objections.

Accordingly, I went with him to see them. They did object most strongly, on the ground that the Queen had liked the Anthem and that it had been used both in the Mausoleum and at Whippingham in the Memorial Services.

I reminded them that this had caused much discussion, as the Queen's use of it on those occasions had everywhere been quoted as giving an official sanction to Prayers for the Dead.[34] We Bishops had had more than once to point out that they were private services, and that no authority had been given for the use of this Anthem at a public service.

But the Funeral at Windsor would be a great national occasion, and the eyes of all the world would be turned to what we did. The use of this Anthem would rejoice many, and others would deplore and denounce it. Was it desirable to make the occasion one of such controversy?

The King, who had made me state my case first, backed me up most strongly, and the Princesses then gave way. The music was already being printed, and by a telephonic master-stroke we telegraphed to the Lord Chamberlain's office the whole words of an alternative Anthem to be printed instead, and all was settled between Osborne and London in five minutes.

Probyn[35] and others were specially delighted afterwards that this had been done, as they felt the harm that would ensue were the King to seem to make a demonstration of this sort at the first of his great services. I had to keep on assuring them all that personally I had no objection to such petitions, and that I was speaking merely in the interests of the King to avoid controversy. The King said repeatedly, '*I see. What you want to protect is the Nonconformist conscience*' I said he might put it so without being far wrong. Anyhow it was a near shave.

---

34 The practice of praying for the dead alongside the doctrine of purgatory had been rejected during the Reformation and it was during the Anglo-Catholic movement of the nineteenth century that attempts were made to reintroduce them. In public, prayers for the dead first began to appear in 1900 for those killed on military service in South Africa. This practice was resisted by both the Church establishment and the evangelicals.

35 Sir Dighton Probyn, Comptroller and Treasurer to the Prince of Wales and his most trusted courtier.

Sir Frederick Ponsonby

Knollys and Greville had practically taken over the whole of the secretarial work and therefore there was no reason why I should remain at Osborne, but when on my return I asked whether anything had been decided about the funeral at Windsor, I was told that nothing of any sort had come from the Earl Marshal's office about Windsor as they were still concentrating on the London part.

I naturally became anxious in case it was supposed that I was doing the funeral procession as well as the arrangements of troops, police, etc, I determined to go to London and make sure what was expected of me.

Lord Edward Pelham-Clinton

Very cold, but bright sunshine.

Twelve of the Royal Family; the younger members, leave at 1 o'clock. A large number of people visit the Chapelle Ardente. Walk for a short time with Breadallon who comes down to see the Chapelle. The King returns from London about 4.45. Prince Ed. of Saxe Weimar,[36] Pss Frederica of Hanover and Baron Rammingen, Prince Frederick of Mecklenburg-Strelitz, Princess Francis and Alexander of Teck and Lady Lytton[37] arrive.

Royal dinner 27. Household dinner of 20.

36 Prince Edward of Saxe-Weimar (1823–1902), nephew of Queen Adelaide and one of Queen Victoria's childhood playfellows.

37 Edith, Countess of Lytton (1841–1936). Lady of the Bedchamber to Queen Victoria and later to Queen Alexandra.

Thursday, 31 January

London

Lord Edward Pelham-Clinton

I leave Osborne by the 9.20 boat, with Fritz Ponsonby and go to 81 Eccleston Square to lunch, then to Pulford and Truefitt (hair cut) and take the 5.5 train to Windsor. Very busy arranging rooms and answering telegrams etc.

Sir Frederick Ponsonby

A second time I rushed off to London and went at once to the Earl Marshal's office where I found absolute chaos.

The Heralds, who claimed the right to manage the funeral under the direction of the Earl Marshal, had little precedent to work on since there had been no Sovereign's funeral for sixty-four years, and being accustomed to work out coats of arms and genealogical tables at their leisure, were swept off their feet with the urgent arrangements for the funeral. There appeared to be no system and everyone was engaged in working out the little bits of detail most suited to their capacity.

I asked for the programme of the Windsor part of the funeral and was told that they had not yet begun it '*We haven't finished Osborne and London yet*', cried one of them. '*But*', I argued, '*has it occurred to you that the funeral starts from Osborne tomorrow?*' I suddenly realised that the Windsor part would be a fiasco, and I should be blamed.

Finding everything so confused I asked to see the Duke of Norfolk, the Earl Marshal, and here I found a thoroughly businesslike and capable man dealing with telegrams, letters, ceremonials, enquiries from the Lord Chamberlain, Lord Steward, Master of the Horse, telephone messages from the Foreign, India, and

Colonial Offices, but quite unconscious that the work he was delegating to his subordinates was not being done.

Although he was working like a cart-horse he at once saw me. He was under the impression that a skeleton programme was being made out and that all that was necessary was to fill in the names, but I explained that nothing had even been started. He seemed rather put out about this and explained that the Lord Chamberlain was constantly supplying him with fresh Kings and Princes who were to attend the funeral, and this made any definite printing of a ceremonial impossible. He said that the best plan would be for me to consult Lord Roberts and then make out a skeleton ceremonial for his approval.

So off to the War Office I went, but when I got to the Commander-in-Chief's room I was told that Lord Roberts could see no one. I, however, wrote on my card, '*Funeral arrangements – urgent*'. I was at once ushered in and I briefly explained that the funeral began at Osborne the next day and that nothing had been decided about the Windsor part. Lord Roberts said that he had nothing to do with the funeral itself, but if it came to giving orders to any troops, I had his permission to give whatever orders were necessary, and say that they were given with his approval.

This was excellent, and I returned to the Earl Marshal's office and sent for a shorthand writer, who told me that it was the first time he had been employed.

It was astonishingly difficult to dictate a programme with practically nothing to go on, but I kept everything in categories: English Royal Family, Foreign Sovereigns, Foreign Princes, Representatives of Foreign Countries, Foreign Suites, etc. Apparently it was impossible to get any accurate lists on account of the constant changes. I think I covered the ground pretty well and let everyone know what they had to do.

When this was typed I took it to the Duke of Norfolk, who made some corrections. He said that some of the Heralds had complained of my rudeness and had resented some remarks on their inefficiency which I had made. I at once apologized to him, but I pointed out that had I not come to London no arrangements of any sort, no orders for the battery of the Horse Artillery, for the Life Guards, Foot Guards, Naval Guard of Honour, would have been issued. He asked me who was now going to give the orders, and I told him that Lord Roberts had given me *carte blanche*.

I told my shorthand friend to have this skeleton ceremonial printed and sent to the various authorities concerned and then went to the Admiralty and War Office to see that the orders were understood.

I returned to Osborne that night and arrived at 2 a.m.

Almeric Fitzroy

In issuing the invitation '*to assist at the interment*' of the late Queen, curious oversights were permitted. Thus, Lord Cadogan[38] showed me his invitation, wherein it was Lady Cadogan, and not he, who was asked to come '*in trousers*', a circumstance to which I called the Earl Marshal's attention when he was chaffing me about some alleged misadventure on the part of the Privy Council.

Osborne House

Randall Davidson, Bishop of Winchester

We had another fairly quiet day, but a great many detailed arrangements had to be made about the Windsor proceedings. At 6.15 we again had a musical Service in the little Chapel. The Choir did even better than before, and everyone was moved. The Household were invited to be present and were in the Drawing Room adjoining with the doors open.

38 George Cadogan, 5th Earl Cadogan and first Mayor of Chelsea.

Then came another little altercation about the Windsor arrangements.

Madame Albani[39] had asked the King to allow her to sing an Anthem in St George's on Sunday, and Parratt had consented to let her do so. I felt this would be a most unfortunate arrangement. Not only would it be the first occasion of a professional singer (a lady) taking a solo in St George's at a Sunday Service, but Madame Albani is a Roman Catholic.

So I took Parratt to the King to see what we could do. The King said he had promised Albani, and then I suggested that as Albani's special wish had been to sing in the place where the Queen's coffin was actually lying, we might offer her instead of St George's the opportunity of singing in the Memorial Chapel on Sunday at a special Service while the coffin was actually there, and that only the Royal Family should be present. She would regard this as a much greater honour, and St George's would not have the innovation.

After some demur the King consented, and ultimately it was carried out in the way I proposed, and Albani was delighted.

39 Emma Albani, Canadian opera singer and favourite soprano of the Queen.

Act V

Rest in Peace

1–4 February 1901

Friday, 1 February

Osborne House

Randall Davidson, Bishop of Winchester

I was early at Osborne, after seeing E.M.D. off from Kent House for Windsor, with Parratt and the boys and Lady Edwards. After breakfast I had a long walk with the Bishop of Ripon and much talk. He then left. Then a further interview with the King about matters on which he wished details to be arranged.

The Funeral Procession was to start at 1.30.

Sir Frederick Ponsonby

I had to get up very early and put on full-dress uniform. Arthur Davidson[1] had been put in charge of all the funeral arrangements at Osborne, and I must say it was beautifully arranged. Everyone knew what to do and where to go. We Equerries were to march on either side of the gun-carriage and to assemble at the front entrance of Osborne House.

Randall Davidson, Bishop of Winchester

Soon after 12.30 Clement Smith and I went to the Chapel and superintended the final arrangements as to the cushions, etc, for the coffin, bearing the crown, sceptre, and orbs. Then we were left alone in the Chapel for half an hour before the men came

1 Lieutenant-Colonel Arthur Davidson, equerry to Queen Victoria, and former aide-de-camp to Field Marshal, the Duke of Cambridge.

to remove the coffin. I felt this to be as solemn a time as any we had had.

At 1.30 the coffin was removed into the Hall at the foot of the Queen's Staircase opposite the large entrance. After a time the Royal Family all gathered there, and we had again a short Service – 'Nunc Dimittis,' 'Prevent us,' a Lesson from St. John, and a few special Prayers. Then the body was carried out.

Sir Frederick Ponsonby

Punctually the bluejackets from the Royal yacht, under Lieutenant Pelly, carried the coffin and placed it on the gun-carriage.

Duke of Argyll

The winter's sun shone brightly as the mourners formed up behind the gun-carriage which had been driven by the artillerymen under the portico where she had so lately gone forth for her drives about the island. The princes in uniform, the princesses walking behind them, and all on foot, passed from the door out to the long avenue of ilex the boughs of which now all but meet above the broad roadway to the entrance gates.

Sir Frederick Ponsonby

The Queen's Company marched in single file on either side of the procession and the whole cortege moved in slow time.

Duke of Argyll

Thence down the hill to the red-roofed town and to the banks of the Medina, and so on board her little yacht, the Alberta, which she had used so often in crossing from and to the mainland.

Randall Davidson, Bishop of Winchester

Clement Smith and I (not in robes, but with ribbons, medals, etc.) walked with the late Queen's Household, immediately behind the ladies, to Trinity Pier. Then he returned home, wishing to conduct the Saturday Service in his own Church, and I embarked with the Household on the 'Victoria and Albert'.

Sir Frederick Ponsonby

It was a lovely still afternoon and the immense crowd was most impressive.

Duke of Argyll

At the mouth of the river was the guard-ship, the Australia, which was to give the signal for the fleet's salute. There, stretched away to the eastward from that guardship, the magnificent array of battle-ships and cruisers lay upon the waters to the distant horizon off Portsmouth. For leagues along the gray wintry waters the line of the British fleet was visible, and far off, near Ryde, could be seen other warships, apart from the regular rank of the floating forts that lay so low and so darkly on the silver tide. These others were the ships of the Germans, and yet another powerful vessel under the command of a gallant French admiral.

Cecilia, Countess of Denbigh

Cecilia Clifford. Married Viscount Feilding, later 9th Earl of Denbigh in 1884.

I went on the *Scot,* where both Houses were embarked. We steamed out and took up our position between the last British ship and the first foreign ships of war, on the south side of the double line down which the procession was to pass. The day was one of glorious sunshine, with the smoothest and bluest of seas.

Cosmo Lang, Vicar of Portsea

Portsmouth Harbour

I went to the Fort at the entrance of the harbour. The two long shores converging on the harbour bar were crowded by masses of people, all in black. There was the strangest silence I have ever known. It could literally be felt. It was so deep and tense that when two children talked at a distance of some 300 yards it seemed an intolerable intrusion. It was a beautiful day, a day of summer rather than of January, the sky clear and the sea blue.

Cecilia, Countess of Denbigh

After a while a black torpedo destroyer came dashing down the line signalling that the Alberta was leaving Osborne.

Cosmo Lang, Vicar of Portsea

Portsmouth Harbour
Suddenly the silence was broken. A sound smote upon the heart. It was the sound of the guns from Osborne across the water telling that the Queen's body was being saluted by the Fleet.

Duke of Argyll

As the salute proceeded, came the flash and report from one ship after another along that line of eleven miles, the minute-guns answering from ironside to ironside, and then flashing and rolling forth again their thunder from the west to the east in continuous shocks of sound.

Cosmo Lang, Vicar of Portsea

Portsmouth Harbour
Then, through the long lines of battleships, stretching in a curve from Cowes to Portsmouth, came the little yacht *Alberta* bearing the body. The yacht was preceded by six torpedo-destroyers moving black and silent like dark messengers of Death sent to summon the Queen. The *Alberta* – small, slight, but dignified, passing through the huge ironclads, seemed strangely like the Queen herself.

I shall never forget the booming of the great guns as the little ship with its precious freight moved slowly down the lines. The sound was varied only by the strains of Chopin's Funeral March, played by each ship's band as the body passed.

Cecilia, Countess of Denbigh

We could see the motionless figures standing round the white pall which, with the crown and orb and sceptre, lay upon the coffin. Solemnly and slowly, it glided over the calm blue water giving one a strange choke, and a catch in one's heart as memory flew back to her triumphal passage down her fleet in the last Jubilee review. As slowly and as silently as it came the cortege passed away into the haze.

Duke of Argyll

The silver and gray of the sea was clouded with the smoke, which, drifting in a haze that became golden as the sun declined, was brightened by stronger light near Portsmouth, whose people, in dense, black, silent masses, fringed all the shore. They then made out the little yacht with its bright standard, ahead of the two larger vessels, the Osborne and the Victoria and Albert, which in turn were ahead of the great gray Hohenzollern, the floating palace of the German Emperor. All glided slowly into harbor, passing Nelson's old flag-ship.

Cosmo Lang, Vicar of Portsea

Portsmouth Harbour

Then – the most moving thing of all – just as the *Alberta* entered the harbour, the sun set in a rich glow of tranquil glory. I heard an old General behind me cough, clear his throat, and say as it were to himself, '*H'm; nothing will persuade me that Providence didn't arrange that!*' So the sun set over the haven where the Queen would be.

Randall Davidson, Bishop of Winchester

The scene crossing the Solent was beyond question the most solemn and moving of which I have ever had experience. The 'Alberta' gliding silently out of sight into Clarence Yard just as the sun set and the gloom of evening fell. I do not envy the man who could pass through such a scene dry-eyed.

Lady Edith Lytton

Travelling with the Queen's coffin on HMY Alberta.

No words can express the beauty of the day. The colour of the Crown, the Royal Standard (and) Union Jack put in perfect folds – the white & gold satin pall over the coffin all looked so splendid & then all the uniforms. Only the Princesses & ladies were in the dreary black & very bad it looked.

Mary, Duchess of Cornwall and York

One of the saddest finest things I have ever seen, a mixture of great splendour and great simplicity, a never to be forgotten sight on the most perfect of sunny days.

London

Mary Monkswell

3.30 p.m. I have just been up St. James's St. & Piccadilly. Most of the houses are hung with purple, & on all the lamp posts hang great round wreaths of evergreens. This decoration is quite a new idea, & was carried out by a Miss Close, who lives in Eaton

Square. She writes to the 'Times' that hundreds of these wreaths arrived directly she asked for them '*from the highest of the land to the very lowest, some of whom carried theirs many miles*'. I think that is lovely.

The Times

The first objects that attract the eye are the dark green wreaths suspended from the lamp posts. This happy idea originated with Miss Etta Close, of 101, Eaton-square. Miss Close formed a committee of ladies, and issued an appeal for wreaths. The response to the appeal has been most remarkable. By Wednesday night garlands more than sufficient for the 800 lamps along the line of route were received, and they were hung up early yesterday morning. But all day yesterday the wreaths still poured in.

At the mews where they were directed to be sent, wreaths filled the stables to overflowing, and piles of them stood in the lane outside. These offerings were contributed by all classes of persons – peers and members of the House of Commons, costers and agricultural labourers, school children and students of Universities, and came from every part of Great Britain. One was from an officer's widow whose husband fought for the Queen in the Crimea and the Indian Mutiny, another came from a rural village to which every inhabitant contributed a sprig of laurel or palm or ivy. All day long wreaths were delivered in railway vans, in hand-carts, in private carriages, by hand, in donkey carts. It was decided by the ladies to hang a second wreath on every lamp-post and to distribute the surplus of the 3,000 garlands received among the hospitals.

The Mourning in the Streets

All day thousands of people traversed the line of route across London by which Queen Victoria is to be conveyed on her last journey through her capital on the way to her place of rest.

The three miles and a half that lie between Victoria Station and the terminus of the Great Western at Paddington presented an unbroken spectacle of animation.

Shopkeepers were emptying their windows of goods and fitting up seats; stands for spectators were being erected on the footways; balconies were being shored up with wooden supports; and, above all, the fronts of business premises and private residences were being swathed with emblems of grief. The dominant tone of the draperies, in obedience to the King's wishes, is purple, the distinguishing colour of potentates, relieved by fringes or festoons of white.

At Victoria Station no trappings are visible; but the huge pillars that support the roof have been repainted, and the staring pictorial advertisements have been removed. Conspicuous on No. 4 platform is a handsome pavilion which has been erected for the accommodation of the King, the German Emperor, and the other Royal mourners while the coffin of the Queen is being removed from the train. When the white and purple hangings of the entrance are drawn back a tastefully furnished apartment is disclosed, with carpets and rugs, the walls being hung with pictures; and standing prominently in the centre is a large pedestal with a marble bust of the Queen draped in purple.

Around Buckingham Palace

With regard to the price of seats, in Buckingham Palace-road the lowest price on the stands was 2 guineas. It was possible to get a place on stands erected in the side streets for a guinea; but seats in the shop windows of the main thoroughfare ranged from five to ten guineas.

In St James's-street the windows of all the houses had seats to let. The price of a seat, whether behind a plate glass window or on a stand, seemed to be everywhere five guineas. In reply to a question asked at one place whether nothing cheaper was to be obtained, it was said that standing room would be given for three guineas on the door-steps of a private house.

Memorial cards in a variety of designs were sold by hawkers for a penny; rosettes of crape and purple buttons with portraits of the Queen with mourning borders and programmes of the procession were to be had at the same price; and for all these mementoes there was a brisk demand.

Piccadilly and Hyde Park

But in Piccadilly the scene was even more busy and more animated. Here the prices of seats run highest. In the windows of a shop at the corner of Albemarle-street, commanding a view of both St. James's street and Piccadilly, the front seats were ten guineas and the back seats five guineas. All the seats of a balcony fronting the first-floor windows were let at 25 guineas. Only one place, in the far corner of the balcony was unengaged, and that could be had for 15 guineas. When it was asked whether breakfast was included the answer was that every one must bring his own morning meal.

It was mentioned also that £500 had been paid for front rooms in a neighbouring hotel. Down the side streets five guineas were asked for a place on the balconies and ten guineas for a window.

Up Edgware-road, where the procession will pass on emerging from Hyde Park, the announcement (Seats to Let) meets the eye at every turn. In one instance it is made more attractive by the statement that '*the advantages of sitting-room, fire, and other comforts*' are included. Even the roofs of the houses are to let here. A placard on a man's back tells where '*good roof view cheap*' may be obtained. A guinea only was asked for this position. The prices, otherwise, were practically the same as in Buckingham Palace-road.

In this district the three borough councils who have control of the route have provided them-selves with stands.

Bringing the Troops to London

About midday a large body of military cooks arrived in London from Aldershot, the proportion being one cook for every 100 men.

According to the instructions received from the War Office the total number of troops who will be engaged in keeping the streets will be 33,000, and of these 25,331 are to be catered for at 28 centres all over London, whilst others will be at various barracks.

The amount of provisions for the troops is about 90,000lb. weight. Breakfast will consist of meat sandwiches and tea, dinner of large meat pies, roll and butter and cheese, with a pint of beer or ginger beer for each man. The order was increased by supplies for several thousand more troops at a late hour on Thursday night, but by 2 o'clock [this] afternoon everything was at the various depots, and the large staff of waiters, consisting of about 500 men, were at their positions ready for duty.

Earl Marshal's Office

The Funeral Trains to Windsor

We are requested to state that since the printing of the letters of invitation the hour for the ceremony in St. George's Chapel has been altered from 1 o'clock to 2 o'clock.

> The following arrangements have been made for special trains:—
>
> Special trains for invited guests will leave Paddington at 12 noon for Windsor. The special train for foreign representatives and for the Corps Diplomatique will leave at 12 30. The special train bearing the Royal remains and the trains conveying those who have taken part in the procession in London will leave at 1 o'clock.
>
> For the above trains no tickets are required on production of a letter of invitation to St. George's Chapel; nor will tickets be required by those who have taken part in the procession in London.

Those who have tickets for admission to the Chapel, but without any letter of invitation, must proceed to Windsor by ordinary trains at hours earlier than those specified above.

The Earl Marshal regrets extremely that, owing to the enormous number of applications and communications and the pressure of time, it has been found impossible to send replies to very many who have communicated with him.

WINDSOR

Lord Edward Pelham-Clinton, Windsor

Very busy all day, constant telegrams altering arrangements for rooms by sending more Royalties. I begin almost to despair of succeeding, but think all is settled. I get out for a few minutes to go to St George's and to ask Lady Bigge[2] if she can take in any of the suite – to my great relief she takes in three. Have all meals by myself in my room.

PORTSMOUTH

Sir James Reid

To his wife, Susan

Royal Yacht Osborne, Portsmouth.
Here I am on board the Osborne feeling rather tired, but happily with nothing to do except write to my Pussy! Everything went

2 Constance Bigge, lady-in-waiting and wife of Sir Arthur Bigge, Queen Victoria's Private Secretary.

off most satisfactorily, and it was fortunate the day was so fine – 'Queen's weather'! I tried to see you on the beach at Osborne, but could not make you out: however, the crowds of people on steamboats and along Southsea beach were wonderful, more than I have ever seen here before. On arriving here about 4.45 (we came very slowly), the Osborne lot left the Victoria and Albert and came on board here; Edwards, Bigge, Fritz, Domestique, Lady Lytton, Gleichen, etc.

Sir Frederick Ponsonby

I was on board the *Osborne*, where I found a cabin prepared for me.

About seven o'clock King Edward sent for me and I went in a steam pinnace to the *Victoria & Albert*. He said he wished me to undertake the arrangements for the final service in the Mausoleum at Frogmore on Monday, and he hoped I should be able to have a printed ceremonial ready for him to see on Sunday morning.

There I was at Portsmouth on board the *Osborne* with nothing to refer to, no precedent to go by, and no idea of who would attend this last ceremony. I was to walk with the other Equerries alongside the gun-carriage through London [tomorrow], and yet I had not only to stage-manage the final ceremony, but also to have a ceremonial printed.

I was dead tired, having been all day on the go with very little sleep the night before. I realised that the next day all the shops would close early to enable people to see the funeral and that the day after was Sunday. Up to that moment Arthur Davidson had managed everything so well that he had set a very high standard and I felt that there was every possibility of the Windsor part being a fiasco. If in addition to this I mismanaged the final ceremony, what little chance I had of being taken on by King Edward would evaporate.

When I grasped all the difficulties I felt I had undertaken a hopeless task, but of course there was no alternative but to tackle it.

It occurred to me that if I was to have anything printed by Monday, the printers must be warned, and I therefore sent a telegram to Oxley, the printer at Windsor, saying I would want a ceremonial printed by Saturday evening and that he was to meet a messenger whom I was sending by an early train and receive from him the written ceremonial.

I sent for one of the King's Home Service Messengers and told him to come to my cabin early the next morning, by which time I would have written out a draft. As the King told me that only those who were staying at Windsor would attend the last ceremony, I grasped that it would be quite a different list from that of the larger ceremony through London. The only possible way I could think of to obtain a correct list was to telegraph to the Master of the Household's clerk at Windsor Castle and ask him to telegraph the names of all those who would be staying in the Castle.

After dinner I retired to my cabin, where I proceeded to write out a ceremonial in suitable language. Under ordinary circumstances I should never have attempted such a thing, but there seemed to be no alternative, and although in some places it seemed rather bald, I succeeded in producing a dignified programme for the printer.

Late that night I received a sheaf of pink telegraph forms giving me, as I had asked, the names and precedence of the guests staying at Windsor for the final ceremony. I filled in all the names and sealed up my draft ready for the Messenger.

SATURDAY, 2 FEBRUARY

Court Circular

His Royal Highness the Duke of Cornwall and York continues to progress satisfactorily.

Cosmo Lang, Vicar of Portsea

Portsmouth Harbour
Very early, about 7 a.m., I went out to the *Alberta* as she lay off the Clarence Pier with the Admiral (Sir Michael Culme-Seymour[3]) in his pinnace. It was a very different day, raining, cold and squally.

After robing in a cabin I had to wait some time till all the Royalties assembled.

The last to arrive was the German Emperor. His arrival was characteristic: out from the side of the great *Hohenzollern* shot a steam launch. The Admiral, who was standing beside me, said: '*Yes, that is the Emperor steering; he expects to bring her alongside; he doesn't know the tide or the currents*.' On came the launch, swaying hither and thither with the currents, but with admirable precision and without the loss of a second the Emperor steered her exactly alongside, threw aside the rudder-cords, and stepped up the steps looking every inch an Emperor.

Only the Royal Family with the Kaiser were present at the service. At its close, when all had left for the train and before the sailors came to carry out the bier, I was the only witness of an episode which I have every reason to remember vividly.

The new King, Edward VII, a man always of warm emotion, paused for a minute or two and knelt silently at the foot of the coffin. The Emperor, turning round, saw this, and quietly knelt at the King's side. The German Emperor and the English King kneeling together, side by side, by the body of Queen Victoria – how could I fail to think, what effect may this have upon the future relations of England and Germany?

Then followed an experience which moved me more deeply than I can express. It had been arranged that officers of the Navy and Army might volunteer to form a Guard of Honour lining the long-covered passage from the yacht to the train. It fell to me to walk in my robes immediately in front of the coffin. I could

3 Former Commander-in-Chief at Portsmouth and principal aide-de-camp to the Queen.

therefore see the faces of these men who had served or fought for the Queen in all parts of the world, as they turned towards her body to give their last salute. I do not think there was one of them who had not tears in his eyes, and certainly there were tears in mine.

The train glided slowly out of the station; and Queen Victoria passed out of sight.

LONDON

Mary Monkswell

Victoria Station

A most wonderful day. Dull & cold, but no rain or snow. I had a seat in Henri's shop about 150 yards from Victoria Station. I got through the crowd quite easily, but various other members of the family never got to their seats at all in the same house, & had to be content with seeing the procession from the pavement. The side streets which led into the route were guarded by cavalry & the route itself lined with soldiers.

Lady Violet Cecil,

Buckingham Gate

George[4] was very excited at the prospect of seeing the Queen's funeral, and the thought of seeing all the Kings and Princes. The one he was keenest about was the King of Greece, '*Because he went to that famous Siege and because the Heroes come from his country*.'

I was called at 7.30 and hurried up and round to fetch George who was at Olive's.[5]

---

4 George Gascoyne-Cecil. Age 5. Violet Cecil's eldest son and grandson of Lord Salisbury, he was killed at the opening of the First World War, age 18.

5 Olive Hermione Maxse, Violet's sister.

All London was in the streets, hurrying in omnibuses and cabs and on foot to see the last of the Queen. We got to Frances Horner's[6] (2 Buckingham Gate) before nine. The troops were already lining the streets and the crowd was dense. Such a crowd. Well dressed, all in black.

From Buckingham Gate one can see the sweep out into St. James's Park in front of Buckingham Palace and there stood the Queen's people, silent, waiting.

A good many people were at the Horners: Mary Elcho[7] with two babies, the boy absurdly like Elcho.[8] I always think it must be fun for Mary having lots of children like Elcho. Yvo[9] is very observant and has a penetrating voice. '*Mama, Mama, there's a soldier giving his gun to a lady*', laughter in the crowd and confusion on the part of the soldier whose officer glared at him.

Constance, Lady Battersea

The eldest child of Sir Anthony de Rothschild, banker and financier. She married Cyril Flower, the Liberal politician, in 1877; he was created Baron Battersea in 1892.

Marble Arch

When I drew up the blinds of my bedroom at an early hour of the morning, I noted with astonishment the appearance of Oxford Street and the Park, where lines of black-clothed women had already taken up their places. Not a colour to be seen, an extraordinary hush seemed to prevail. Our friends began to arrive early and took up their positions in the gallery; my husband left me to

6 Frances Horner, society hostess and muse of Edward Burne-Jones.

7 Mary Charteris, Lady Elcho, the eldest of the Wyndham sisters and lover of Arthur Balfour and Wilfred Scawen Blunt; married to Lord Elcho.

8 Hugo Charteris, Lord Elcho, son of the 10th Earl of Wemyss.

9 Yvo Charteris. Age 4. Son of Lord and Lady Elcho.

receive them, as his official duties took him to the station, there to await the arrival of the cortège.

Kate Frye

Edgware Road

It [a grocer's shop] had all been boarded in – the big round step and the two skylights in front and at the side so there was lots of room and it was quite private. The window had been let to a party – Mr Hunt's friends took the two skylights – we and another lady had the step – till the five chance customers who had bought the only seats sold turned up then they had the front behind the barrier. We all saw most perfectly.

Mary Monkswell

Victoria Station

The streets were indeed a strange sight, thronged with chiefly decent, respectable, & middle-aged people, every one of them in mourning. Looking down from my window, even by 9 o'c there did not seem room for another person on the pavement. We had the greatest interest in seeing various troops march past that were going to take their place in the procession. As far as I could see along the route, just under the Riding School, were some Horse Artillery & a khaki-coloured field gun that had passed us about 9.30 to get into its place. It made us feel very bad to see coming out of the Royal Mews about 10.30, the eight cream-coloured ponies with their magnificent trappings of purple & gold drawing the khaki-coloured gun-carriage with the gun looking out behind to carry our dear Queen's coffin.

Lady Violet Cecil

Buckingham Gate
George was very happy. He stood for hours quite still, was tired, but nothing would induce him to leave the balcony or sit down. He regarded standing as a point of honour and when Mary Elcho, exhausted, sat on the floor, he turned fiercely on her and said, '*You are cheating*.' I sat inside during most of the long wait.

Mary Monkswell

Victoria Station
We saw all the Kings & Princes riding horses, & the 4 or 5 shut carriages for Queen Alexandra & the Princesses, pass up to the Station.

A little later came Lord Roberts riding; he was the only person the people thought they might cheer, so he got a quiet cheer from everybody as he came along.

Lady Violet Cecil

Buckingham Gate
Presently 'Bobs'[10] rode by with his staff. The crowd gave a muffled cheer. The dear little man made no response at all. Then Ministers and strange Foreign Officials began to go by towards Victoria Station, and we found we were very ignorant of foreign uniforms.

Duke of Argyll

Victoria Station
Here, past the ranks of troops in great coats, fringing the roadway which they kept clear, the King, the German Emperor, the

10 Field Marshal Earl Roberts, Commander-in-Chief British Army.

princes, and others rode, cloaked and plumed, carriages conveying the princesses, while officers of the household and others marched on foot.

George, Duke of Cambridge

Victoria Station
I drove to Victoria Station with Prince Edward[11] and Dolly, and there joined all the Kings and Royalties.

Sir Frederick Ponsonby

Victoria Station
We all stood waiting with the King and the male members of the Royal Family for this train to come in.

Sir James Reid

Victoria Station
There was an imposing assemblage at Victoria Station, and a little confusion until the Procession was arranged and started.

George, Duke of Cambridge

Victoria Station
The Royal train with the Queen's Body arrived at 11.

---

11 Prince Edward of Saxe-Weimar (1823–1902), nephew of Queen Adelaide and one of Queen Victoria's childhood playfellows.

Sir Frederick Ponsonby

Victoria Station

The coffin was carried by men of the Coldstream on to the gun-carriage with the Equerries on either side.

Constance, Lady Battersea

Marble Arch

We sat in a state of trembling excitement, until the booming of the guns came as the first herald of the approach. I seemed to feel the wind blow colder at that moment, whilst some black and threatening clouds looked like the harbingers of a fleeting snow-storm.

Lady Violet Cecil

Buckingham Gate

We were a long way down the line of the procession. Soon a staff officer rode by at a canter and, after a little while, the troops which had taken up their position in the procession opposite to us began to move off in slow time and we knew that the Queen had come to London for the last time.

Mary Monkswell

Victoria Station

About 11.30 I saw the signallers, placed at intervals of about 100 yards shake their signal flags, & the procession began the slow march – so slow, extraordinarily slow, as if each lagging footstep trod upon our hearts.

Sir James Reid

Procession
I walked on the left side of the gun carriage behind the aides-de-camp, and just in front of Davidson – a very slow march.

George, Duke of Cambridge

Procession
I drove in the fourth carriage with Edward Weimar and Lord Wolseley.[12] The crowds were very enormous, but their demeanour magnificent, solemn and silent.

The Standard

Procession
They moved with a mournful slowness. The feet of the men seemed to fall on the sanded road as though they walked on velvet; their right hands were clasped on the butts, the left hand on the barrels of their reversed rifles. They advanced stiff and rigid, animated figures of grief.

Silence hung like a pall over the breathless crowd, a silence oppressive and painful. It was a relief when the Field Artillery with a battery of six guns came by, and the jingle of chains, the rattle of wheels and the tramp of horses broke the spectral stillness. There was more sound as the Lancers, the Hussars and the Dragoons came clinking along, and then the Household Cavalry, massive and majestic. Behind them came the infantry and then a detachment of Bluejackets, who disdained all wrappings and strode along, brawny and strong, in straw hats and thin blue shirts that made chilly landsmen on balconies shiver to look at them.

12 Garnet Wolseley, 1st Viscount Wolseley, Gold Stick in Waiting.

Next appeared the Headquarters Staff and Lord Roberts, riding alone with an orderly behind him, alert, erect, casting his supervising glance around, a true chief of men.

And now the beat of slow music was heard from a great orchestra, the massed bands of the Guards, of the Royal Engineers and the Royal Artillery. The passionate sadness of Chopin's Funeral March fell upon our ears as it throbbed from the muffled drums and wailed softly from the wind instruments. As its solemn harmonies died away in the distance, the painful hush again fell on the multitude for they knew it heralded the crowning stage of the cortege.

And presently it came into sight, and almost an audible exclamation of surprise stole from the lips of beholders. For after the long train of dark and warlike figures on which we had been gazing, the bier itself was like a beautiful jeweller's work, a thing that seemed to speak not of despair but of light, of hope, of serenity.

Lady Violet Cecil

Buckingham Gate
Opposite our balcony was the colour of a regiment dressed in crape. As the front man in the escort passed, the colour was lowered and so remained with its silken glory in the dust.

Mary Monkswell

Victoria Station
A troop of 40 or 50 horsemen came first; I did not concern myself much with whom they were, as my eyes were fixed so entirely upon the one great object, that, except for the Prince of Wales, now King, & the Kaiser, who rode a magnificent white horse on his right hand, I saw nothing else, & that I could hardly see because my eyes were filled with tears & I felt very alloverish & shaky.

The Queen's coffin stood high on the gun carriage drawn by the eight cream-coloured ponies. It was covered by a magnificent white satin pall, edged with gold, & embroidered with the Crown & Arms of England. The flag lay over part of it, & on it was the Crown, the Sceptre, & the Orb. Behind it, the Royal Standard was carried, hung with crepe.

Constance, Lady Battersea

Marble Arch

My eyes were arrested by the two principal figures of the day, our own King Edward, and the Kaiser Wilhelm, closely draped in his military coat, the collar of which almost hid his features. I remember remarking the deathly pallor of the German Emperor, and the way he seemed to be nervously evading the cold blast of the February wind.

The coffin reposing on the gun-carriage and covered with the Union Jack looked strangely small and un-regal – yet it was a Queen-Empress being taken to her rest by her soldiers.

Mary Monkswell

Victoria Station

I could not take my eyes off the gleam of the white pall & the Crown as long as I could see it.

Then I silently bid Her farewell. The people stood uncovered & silent, the only sounds were the band playing the Funeral March & the trampling of the horses.

Caroline Holland

Procession

I witnessed the funeral procession, as it passed through London.

The crowds were a marvellous sight to see. But the one point that stands out above all others in memory was the approach of the first sight of the funeral car, I might no doubt from the papers have been better informed, but with the remembrance of the only other public funeral I had seen, the Duke of Wellington's, with its monstrous ungainly car, all draped in black in my mind, I had anticipated vaguely something of the same sort. I was fairly taken by a surprise which seized me by the throat, when the low gun carriage with its little, little burden hove into sight, the tiny coffin draped in softest white satin the whole thing so pure, so tender, so womanly, so suggestive of her who lay sleeping within that every heart, one felt, must needs go out to meet her.

Sir Edward Walter Hamilton

Procession

The procession was so long that it extended all the way from Victoria Station to nearly Devonshire House in Piccadilly. The distances were not kept very well, partly owing to the changes in pace which took place; but on the whole it was a very impressive sight. The two things that struck me most was (1) the King's appearance – he looked 'every inch a King', on his splendid horse, and (2) the behaviour of the crowd, which is believed to have been a record one for London. There was not a sound heard beyond the playing of the funeral march; there was not a head that was not bared; there was no crushing or stampeding.

Kate Frye

Edgware Road

Miles and miles of soldiers – a regal soldier's funeral truly and the most impressive one possible. We could see them coming half the length of the Edgware Road – from the Marble Arch and they looked like some long long wave. The brass helmets then the banners.

I never took my eyes off the coffin whilst it was in sight – as if I couldn't let our Queen go.

Some of the uniforms were magnificent – but the German Emperor had a Field Marshal's uniform as had the King. I do love the Emperor's face – he is so striking – I am glad to have seen him. The King looked round our way – so I saw him well – he looked very pale and puffy but nicer than I expected.

The Standard

Almost before one had grasped its import, the little casket had glided by. And so we looked our last upon the Queen, and even as we did so were reminded that life rolls on remorselessly though the greatest and the best pass away. The Queen was dead but the King lived.

Behind the gun carriage came a giant trooper of the Household Cavalry flaunting aloft in the air the Royal Standard of England. Under its folds rode the King with the German Emperor on his right hand and the Duke of Connaught on his left, both courteously keeping a pace or two behind him, so as to give His Majesty due prominence as the central figure of the whole solemn display. He rode with a kingly dignity. Pale as he was, and worn, with the marks of much recent suffering and anxiety on his face, he looked like the ruler of a mighty empire, the heir of a long line of monarchs.

Lady Violet Cecil

Buckingham Gate

After the carriages had passed and it was all over, there were sharp military orders, the crowd began to shuffle and talk and we realised better what the hush had been. I asked George what he thought of it. He was impressed, '*But I didn't think they would have all those fancy people at a funeral.*' We lunched with the Dawkinses.

Duke of Argyll

Procession
No disorder took place, but the pressure of the crowd was so great that the heavy iron railings of the park gave way before it.

New York Times

It was not to be expected that the day would pass without accidents, and these were very numerous, in spite of the evident desire of all the crowds to be orderly. The St. John's Ambulance Association attended 1,305 persons injured during the crushes. The association had 701 doctors and nurses busy at 26 stations. Individual hospitals admitted as many as thirty cases. Several persons were badly hurt through falling from elevated places. There was an ugly crush in the crowd at the Marble Arch, when the gates were unexpectedly closed after the procession had passed. Several persons fainted. Prior to the arrival of the funeral train, Major Edward Bassindale, a veteran officer, fell dead in the crowd outside Victoria Station, as the result of excitement.

Arnold Bennett

Writer and novelist.

Procession
This morning I saw what I could, over the heads of a vast crowd, of the funeral procession of the Queen. The people were not, on

the whole, deeply moved, whatever journalists may say, but rather serene and cheerful. Afterwards, Legge, Fred Terry, and Hominy, lunched with me at the Golden Cross Hotel, and all was very agreeable and merry.

Sir Frederick Ponsonby

Procession

The streets were lined all the way with troops and the densely massed crowd was a wonderful sight, most reverent and silent. As we marched in slow time it took quite a long time to get to Paddington.

Sir James Reid

Procession

Two hours I think till we reached Paddington, immense crowds all the way, and no end of purple cloth stuck up on balconies, stands, etc, as mourning; not much black. Not a sound anywhere as we passed, and everybody in the crowds looking woebegone.

Almeric Fitzroy

Paddington Station

A great gathering of Ministers, ex-Ministers, their wives, and prominent officials assembled at Paddington to be conveyed to Windsor by the midday special.

Lady Helena Gleichen

Countess Helena Gleichen. Age 28. Her grandmother was Queen Victoria's half sister, Feodora. A painter of animals, horses and landscapes, she was to train and work as a field radiographer during the First World War.

Paddington Station

Our orders were to be at Paddington Station by a certain time. We should there find a special train with seats reserved in it for us.

A mounted policeman was at the front door waiting to precede our carriage through the streets. Smothered from head to foot in crape with long crape veils reaching down to the ground we started for the station with plenty of time to spare.

All went well until we reached the middle of Hyde Park when the policeman's horse suddenly shied violently and sat down. Our horse followed suit; the coachman was unable to pull him up in time, and he climbed on to the other horse's back, and breaking one shaft. The crowd, very solemn up to that moment, were delighted and surged forward with offers of help and pieces of string which were gratefully accepted. Five or ten minutes later, tied up with string like a parcel, we continued our drive to Paddington.

Arrived there we were greeted by officials who put us into a train waiting by the platform and told us that we should be starting almost immediately. The whole station was hung with mourning drapery and a guard of honour was drawn up opposite our carriage. Mounted police rode in, gave messages and rode out again; time went on, our train did not move.

We sent our footman to ask officials if there had been a mistake and if we were in the wrong train. '*No, it's all right, your train will go presently.*' We grew more and more anxious as we knew that by that time we ought to have been sitting in our places in St. George's Chapel. There was nothing to be done, so we gave ourselves up to watching what was going on.

The feeling of expectancy grew stronger and stronger. The train which was to carry the bier was drawn up opposite to ours.

Then we heard the notes of the Dead March, first far away, gradually coming closer and closer. Arms were reversed, the men's heads were bowed and the wail of the bagpipes echoed through the arches of the big station, making an almost unendurable noise, followed by dead silence only broken by the sound of the horses' feet as they came to a stand with the gun-carriage in front of the funeral train.

Duke of Argyll

Paddington Station

Only two trains left the Great Western station for Windsor. One was filled by the ambassadors and other visitors; and the second was the train that included among its cars the Queen's own travelling carriage, which had been made with a wide door to allow her chair to enter during those last years when she could not go far on foot. Alas! now the width of the entrance had made it to be the chosen vehicle for the crimson, blue, and white draped coffin.

Lady Helena Gleichen

Paddington Station

Then all was bustle and hurry, hundreds of different-coloured uniforms hastening to take their places in the trains reserved for them. Red, scarlet, white, gold, every nation represented, the picturesque Hungarians in their Hussar tunics with fur capes thrown over their shoulders, Indians, gorgeous in pale blue, scarlet and gold, with white turbans decorated with marvellous jewels, all hurrying to and fro with anxious faces.

An order to the guard of honour, and as the train bearing the coffin moved out of the station, our train, crowded with officers, pulled slowly out behind it.

No one recognized the two little black figures in the corner of the carriage reserved for foreign guests. What were we to do when the train arrived at Windsor! I remember hating two of the foreigners, who did nothing but laugh as they tidied themselves up for their next appearance. They did not mind a bit and we all minded so much.

The Times

The Royal train which conveyed the coffin of the Queen and the illustrious mourners to Windsor consisted of seven eight-wheel coaches, five saloons and two brake-vans, and was built for her late Majesty's Jubilee in 1897. The Queen's carriage, technically known as 'Royal No. 2' had existed for some years previous as a six-wheeler and was to have been abolished to make room for a new and larger coach. But, as her Majesty had expressed a feeling of attachment to this particular carriage, the railway authorities decided to retain its services, by adding another pair of wheels and 10ft to its length, to harmonize with the construction of the new train. Both the Tsar and the German Emperor have travelled in it, and it was in this particular carriage that the Queen made her last sad journey to Windsor on Saturday.

The sumptuous divans and revolving fauteuils [wooden-framed armchairs] had been removed, and in their place stood an imposing catafalque, about 2ft. high, equipped with four huge white leather straps. The whole was draped in purple and ornamented with white satin rosettes. The interior of the compartment (which had been enlarged by the removal of a partition) was entirely upholstered in white satin. Broad purple stripes divided the walls into panels, crowned with a purple garland and held by white rosettes and ribbons.

Almeric Fitzroy

All along the route, wherever a view of the line could be obtained, crowds of people dressed in black were awaiting the *convoi* of the dead Queen. The sun shone brightly as we came in view of the great pile that so fitly sums up and embalms the past glories of the British Monarchy.

WINDSOR

Clement Williams

I was in the Oxfordshire Light Infantry and I was present at Queen Victoria's funeral. The day was bitterly cold. It was snowing hard and we had to leave Oxford at five o'clock to get there in time.

We caught the train, but there were no heated carriages in those days. When we arrived at Slough, seeing that we had plenty of time in hand, our commanding officer sent us on a twelve-mile march to warm us up. We marched into Windsor, where we were given a tin mug of beer and a pork pie. Then we stood about and waited until the ceremony began.

Nina Halliday

Daughter of Edward Halliday, a master decorator and house builder in Windsor. Age 7 at the time of the funeral.

We saw the procession from a stand which had been erected under the Guildhall. The seats were covered in black material and everyone wore black clothes, but I had a dress, coat and hat of a lovely mauve colour – I loved it. The streets were lined by Foot Guards and the pavements were packed tight with people all dressed in black. It was a long wait, as the train bringing the coffin and all the important people travelled very slowly from Paddington to Windsor – so that people at the stations which it passed could see it.

Clement Williams

St George's Chapel
We lined the route to St George's Chapel but we had nothing to do because the crowds weren't allowed there.

Lady Helena Gleichen

Windsor Station
[Our] train drew into Windsor station, already the coffin had been put on the gun-carriage ready to draw it up to St. George's Chapel. There was a clattering of swords and spurs as the foreign representatives ran to take their places in the procession.

Sir Frederick Ponsonby

Windsor Station
When we arrived at Windsor I at once got hold of David Kinloch, who had done wonders on the very meagre instructions which I had given him. He had arranged everything perfectly and managed to form up the outline of the procession, leaving plenty of room as he had no idea of the numbers.

Almeric Fitzroy

St George's Chapel
A very long wait ensued, which the coldness of the chapel aggravated intensely. A movement of the Archbishop and clergy to the west door, and the minute-guns announcing the arrival of the funeral train at Windsor, for a moment excited expectation, but another long pause, and a still more sombre stillness fell upon the scene.

Lady Helena Gleichen

Windsor Station
Fritz Ponsonby at that moment caught sight of us and called a corporal of Grenadiers, telling him to escort us through the crowd and up to the Chapel as quickly as possible. Stumbling at every step over our long veils, which were not meant for walking in, we hurried after him through the crowd, who parted to let us through.

Sir Frederick Ponsonby

Windsor Station
As soon as the King and the other foreign Sovereigns had taken up their places (they were to walk this time), I went and asked His Majesty's permission to start the funeral procession. It had been previously arranged that I should hold up my hand and the band would begin the Dead March while the officer in charge of the gun-carriage would start at the same time.

When I received the King's commands to start the procession, I stepped out well to the side so that everyone could see me and held up my hand. The drums at once began to roll and the procession started.

The horses on the gun-carriage had, however, been standing still in the cold for some time, and as the lieutenant in charge never gave the command '*Walk march*', the two wheelers suddenly started off before the leaders, and finding an unusually heavy load, began to kick and plunge. Away flew the traces and the gun-carriage remained still. I had contemplated all sorts of things going wrong, but such a mishap had never occurred to me.

James Cecil Dalton

Royal Horse Artillery.

Windsor Station
Lieut. Goldie, was in command and the team had been so long standing at the station in the bitter cold that when the time came to move off the horses got restless and out of hand and the splinter bar was broken and there was nearly a serious accident.

Sir Frederick Ponsonby

Windsor Station
Meanwhile the front of the procession, unconscious that anything was wrong, had slowly marched on and the band had already turned the corner when I sent a non-commissioned officer to stop them.

I found then that the traces were broken and everyone was trying to get the horses clear while several officers were engaged in trying to devise some makeshift, but naturally the first thing was to inform the King of what exactly had happened.

I did so, and on coming away Prince Louis of Battenberg said, '*If it is impossible to mend the traces you can always get the naval guard of honour to drag the gun-carriage*'.

I went back to the horses where I found that it was contemplated getting two horses only to drag the gun-carriage with the leaders' traces. The general impression, however, seemed to be that this was a most hazardous solution of the difficulty as it seemed very doubtful whether the two horses would be able to drag the gun-carriage up the steep hill into the Castle with traces that were only makeshifts, and which might easily snap.

Another solution was suggested, and that was that the gun-carriage should go up by the shortest way to St. George's, but this I dismissed as it would have meant disappointing a crowd of several thousands.

So I determined to adopt Prince Louis's suggestion and accordingly went a second time to the King and said, '*Have I your Majesty's permission to take out the horses and let the men of the naval guard of honour drag the gun-carriage?*' The King said, '*Certainly*.'

I told the captain of the naval guard of honour to pile arms and bring his men up to the gun-carriage.

While he was doing this I went to the officer in charge of the Artillery team and told him to get the horses clear as the men of the naval guard of honour were to take their places. This raised a storm of discussion, all carried on in a whisper. There were several Artillery officers among the A.D.C.s to the Queen who resented very much the orders I had given, and they assured me that all would be well if I would leave things alone.

Bigge was particularly angry and told me I was ruining the whole ceremony as I knew nothing about Artillery horses. I replied that I was merely carrying out the King's orders and that I could not allow anyone to interfere. He was furious, however, and went off to expostulate with the King, who merely said, '*Right or wrong, let him manage everything; we shall never get on if there are two people giving contradictory orders*.'

So all the men of the Artillery stood sulkily looking on while I went in search of a rope, feeling this was a necessity for the sailors.

The stationmaster to whom I applied rushed off and returned with a steel hawser which was all he had. This was, of course, out of the question as it would have cut the men's hands to the bone. The Artillery A.D.C.s were triumphant and said '*You'll have to come back to the horses after all*.' I went to the Officer commanding the naval guard of honour and explained to him the situation. He said that if he could have the remaining traces off the horses he could manage and I told him to order his men to get them. The men of the Artillery remained looking on while the sailors swarmed round the horses and took off the traces. In an incredibly short time they had got into a compact group and were ready to start.

The whole of this lasted about ten to fifteen minutes, but it seemed to me about two hours. I went off to the King and reported that everything was ready, and having received orders to start the procession, I stepped out for the second time and held up my hand. This time all went well.

I returned to my place alongside of the gun-carriage. The procession moved slowly along High Street and Park Street and then turned up towards the Castle through the gates at the bottom of the Long Walk.

Nina Halliday

Windsor Procession

It was a wonderful procession, with the Life and Foot Guards playing the Dead March. The Guard of Honour led; then came the gun carriage covered by the Royal Standard. The new King, Edward VII, followed with many of the Queen's relations and Kings and Princes all in uniform. The finest was the Emperor of Germany in a beautiful white uniform and white helmet with lots of gold on it, and many Orders and decorations. Then came the chiefs of the Navy and Army and members of the Queen's Household, followed by members of the Queen's Court, including her daughters and other relations in royal carriages – all, of course, in black with long veils.

I seem to remember that a purple cushion was on the coffin with a small crown on it. The bands had muffled drums and as the procession came along, one could hear the slow booming of the guns. All very solemn, so much black and such a small coffin – but so much colour as well, with so many uniforms.

Sir Frederick Ponsonby

Windsor Procession

It was very heavy going and the gun carriage seemed to sink in, but the sailors experienced no difficulty. One of the A.D.C's called my attention to the brake and said that if no one understood how to work it there might be serious trouble when we descended the steep hill to St. George's Chapel.

So I moved out of my place and consulted the naval lieutenant, who said he had a petty officer who understood all about the brake, but that if I liked he would place three men on each wheel so that, in the event of the brake not working, there would be no danger of the gun-carriage going too fast downhill. I asked him to do this.

Clement Williams

St George's Chapel

We knew by the salute guns that the coffin must have arrived at Windsor, but it was taking a long time to reach the castle. Time went by and I saw Earl Clarendon, the chap in charge of the ceremony – he kept coming out and looking down the road, wondering why nobody came. You could hear a band in the distance, but nothing was happening. Then Queen Alexandra came tearing out, looking this way and that way, before Clarendon persuaded her to go back into the Chapel.

Lady Helena Gleichen

St George's Chapel

Never did I know a man walk so fast, and we were both completely blown by the time we reached the door of the Chapel, only just in time, one minute before the head of the procession came in sight, Old Spencer Ponsonby was there to meet us, and whispering, '*I thought you had missed your train and have put someone else into your seats*,' he hurried us up to the Altar and turned the other unhappy people out to make room for us.

Duke of Argyll

St George's Chapel

The band of straw hats and white shirts, with the broad, blue, falling collars, drew the heavy burden with ease and certainty to the west door of the great Chapel of St. George.

Except within the Castle, where troops only were allowed to be stationed, there were many people assembled. These had thronged all the day before to see the thousands of beautiful wreaths of flowers sent in token of sorrow to be laid near the Queen. Their blossoms filled all the cloisters and all the grass space enclosed by the cloisters. They made the whole of this plot of ground one bright garden bed of bloom.

Clement Williams

St George's Chapel

Finally, the carriage came along very slowly, hauled along by the Navy.

Almeric Fitzroy

St George's Chapel

At last the west doors were flung open, and up the steep steps was borne the casket containing the dead Queen's body the extreme shortness of it struck one with pathetic insistence; almost a child's coffin this, yet so deep and heavy, and hardly a coffin at all in shape, so near the centre was its widest point.

Rider Haggard

An English novelist and agricultural commentator.

St George's Chapel

This I saw from the house of one of the minor Canons, which was exactly opposite to the steps of the Chapel at Windsor.

The sight of the gorgeous procession passing up those steps impressed itself very deeply on me. The bearers staggering under the weight of the massive leaden coffin that yet seemed so short, till once or twice I thought that they must fall; the cloaked King Edward walking immediately behind, followed by a galaxy of princes; the officer, or aide-de-camp, who came to him, saluting, to make some report or ask some order, and received a nod in answer; the troops with arms reversed; the boom of the solemn guns; the silent, watching multitude; the bright sun gilding the wintry scene; the wind that tossed the plumes and draperies – all these and more made a picture never to be forgotten.

Edmund H. Fellowes

A minor canon at St George's Chapel.

St George's Chapel

We (the clergy and choir) met the procession at the West Door so we saw the blue jackets drawing the gun carriage and also saw the bearer party of the guards carrying the coffin up the steps which they did with the greatest difficulty, magnificent men though they were, and I could see the front man's hand trembling from nervousness when they were in difficulties with the weight.

We fell in behind the heralds and immediately in front of the coffin, and went straight up inside the rails singing the Croft music to the opening sentences. The choir drew up on the south of the Altar and we on the North. The coffin was placed in the centre just outside the rails and the Princes and Kings came in behind, in rows of 3. They extended beyond the choir to the West door.

Sir Frederick Ponsonby

St George's Chapel

We all followed in procession and found the Chapel crowded with people. It subsequently turned out that the Earl Marshal's people had forgotten to give seats in the choir to anyone, but Sir Spencer Ponsonby-Fane to whom the Earl Marshal had entrusted the arrangements in the Chapel, had grasped that a mistake had been made and had taken suitable people from the nave and placed them in the choir.

Duke of Argyll

St George's Chapel

Within St. George's the mass of the congregation was confined to the nave. The invited visitors were in the chancel, the mourners marching in the procession filled the choir as they followed the dead, and streamed in their bright uniforms, filling the central space with colour for their greatcoats had been laid aside as they passed into the candle-lit shadows of the church.

Randall Davidson, Bishop of Winchester

St George's Chapel

The Choir itself was extraordinarily impressive as seen from the Altar. The candles were all lit, and the little lights glimmered like jewels in a dark casket. The stalls were nearly all occupied by Diplomats and great officials in brilliant uniforms. The music was perfect and the whole effect was overwhelming. The Bishop of Oxford, the Dean of Windsor, and I all wore our Garter robes.

A blunder was made about the moment at which we were to start from the Chapter room to the Nave, and in the result the clerical Procession, headed by the two Archbishops and containing all the Clergy and the Choir, was kept standing for forty minutes in the Nave. The Bishop of Oxford[13] was rather unwell afterwards.

Almeric Fitzroy

St George's Chapel
A member of the choir was taken away fainting, and the stalwart figure of the octogenarian Archbishop seemed the only one in the long white procession unaffected by the strain.

Duke of Argyll

St George's Chapel
Glorious music, beloved by the Queen, rose from organ and choristers. The white coffin, with its gleaming crown and orbs, was lifted on to the bier above the throng standing around it. The words of hope and peace and faith of the burial service were said; the herald proclaimed the departure of one mighty sovereign and the accession of King Edward VII, and then gradually the mourners left, and the banners in gorgeous array above the dark carved pinnacles of the chancel walls drooped alone over the Guardsmen, who, in their bearskins and with arms reversed, remained to watch over the dead.

13 Rt Rev. William Stubbs. Died 22 April 1901.

Clement Williams

St George's Chapel

After the ceremony, King Edward VII appeared on the steps of St George's Chapel. He stood with the Kaiser and we gave them the royal salute. They saluted us back. Then they went off and we packed up and went home.

Lady Helena Gleichen

Windsor Castle

Our troubles were not quite over, as thinking we were not coming our places had been filled for luncheon, too, and we went back to London without having had any food of any kind, arriving at home more dead than alive having started out at 8.30 a.m. What a horrid day.

Sir Frederick Ponsonby

Windsor Castle

All the Foreign Sovereigns, Princes and Representatives went up to the Castle, where there was a stand-up buffet, where I was able to get something to eat and drink; but a message that the King wished to see me interrupted my post-prandial moments, and I hurried off to Edward III's Tower, where the King was temporarily lodged.

Almeric Fitzroy

Windsor Castle

It was fully four o'clock before we reached St. George's Hall, where an excellent luncheon was provided for some eight hundred people. I had all I wanted in a very few minutes, and returned to the station with the Duke of Grafton,[14] who told me the Duke of Cambridge had spoken to him very dismally about the Queen's death, and was very much broken by the blow. '*I shall go soon myself,*' he groaned, and to cheer him up the Duke of Grafton said he was nearly as old himself, upon which the old Duke said almost cheerfully, '*Ah! we will both go together.*' We came up with the Duke and Duchess of Abercorn,[15] and reached London about half past five.

Randall Davidson, Bishop of Winchester

Windsor Castle

Extraordinary blunders had been made by either the Earl Marshal or the Lord Chamberlain's department as to the issuing of tickets for the Nave.

They had been sought for from every quarter by all kinds of people, and hundreds had been told that there was no corner for them, whereas in the end the Nave was not much more than half full, the officials having to spread the people out, when the hour drew near, to cover the seats and hide the mistake that had been made.

It was rather sad, but I suppose some blunders are inevitable at such a time. It was said to be partly due to the fact that the procession itself – some 200 or more – had been expected to take seats on arriving in St. George's, and had therefore been furnished with tickets; whereas as a matter of fact they all stood.

The Bishop of Oxford was rather unwell afterwards, and I found Sir Thomas Barlow at the 'Luncheon' (4 p.m.!) in St. George's Hall and took him to see the Bishop. He does not give a very buoyant or hopeful opinion of him. I was thoroughly knocked up, and went to bed at the Norman Tower about 8 p.m.

14 Augustus FitzRoy, 7th Duke of Grafton. Age 79.

15 James and Mary Hamilton, 2nd Duke and Duchess of Abercorn.

George Lappage

Windsor Castle
We went back to barracks and that night three troopers and an officer were told to go up to Windsor Castle and do sentry over the Queen's body.

'I commit to you the charge of the body of her late Majesty Queen Victoria, Queen of Great Britain and Ireland, Empress of India, together with the Regalia of the British Empire.'

I was posted just outside the Chapel door.

Sir Frederick Ponsonby

Windsor Castle
[The King] told me he wished me to do all the arrangements for the final funeral on Monday, and that as the sailors had done so well that day he would like them again to drag the gun-carriage.

I ventured to point out to him that the Artillery had been deeply mortified at their failure that day, coming as it did so soon after the experience at Ladysmith when so much had been made of the handy-man taking the place of the artilleryman, and that therefore they would be much hurt if the sailors took their place again.

He talked it over for some time and said that he had no wish to hurt the feelings of the Artillery. He quite realised that they were not to blame and that it was only an unlucky accident, but he really thought that the sailors had been most effective and had really added to the dignity of the procession. I, however, pressed my point and finally he said, *'Very well, the gun-carriage will be drawn by the Artillery, but if anything goes wrong I will never speak to you again.'*

I was determined that nothing should go wrong and I wrote to Sir Arthur Bigge, Sir Henry Ewart the Crown Equerry, the Officer Commanding the battery of Artillery, the lieutenant in charge of the Artillery team, the captain of the Queen's Company Grenadiers, and asked them to come to the door of St. George's Chapel at 6 a.m. the next morning, Sunday. I told the Artillery to have their team of horses there, and Arthur Lloyd commanding the Queen's Company to have all his men there.

I received charming letters from all of them, but an especially nice and forgiving letter from Bigge saying he was to glad to hear the Artillery were to have another chance and promising to help me in any way he could.

Lord Esher, the Secretary of the Office of Works, suggested that we should have a rehearsal of the final ceremony at the Mausoleum. He asked me to order the bearer party and the gun-carriage and horses to be down at the Mausoleum at eleven that night and he would have a box approximately the same size and same weight as the coffin made by the men of the Office of Works ready at the lodge leading to the Mausoleum.

We drove down in a carriage and found all the men waiting. It was a pitch-dark night and there was something very ghostly about the lanterns that were carried to light up various points. It was a weird scene and the two bearer parties, one from the Life Guards and one from the Foot Guards, remained motionless on the steps of the Mausoleum. The gun-carriage with the Artillery team was standing at the lodge with the box on it and had been told not to move until ordered to do so. Lord Esher had thought of everything and had told the men that all was to be done exactly as it would be on the Monday.

We then began the rehearsal, and the gun-carriage with the sham coffin advanced slowly to the steps of the Mausoleum. It had been arranged that as the coffin was very heavy one bearer party should carry it up two flights of steps and then be relieved by the other bearer party, who would carry it into the Mausoleum.

The first part went very well and the relieving bearer party took over the sham coffin, but when they advanced up the remaining steps, we realised that they would have to place the coffin on the tomb the reverse way to the marble figure of the Prince Consort. We came to the conclusion that this would never do and we halted the men.

While we were discussing what should be done, I noticed that although the bearer party consisted of enormously powerful men they were staggering under the weight of the sham coffin, and I suggested that they should put it back on the gun-carriage while we decided what should be done. The sham box coffin was therefore carried back again and placed on the gun-carriage.

We discussed whether at St. George's Chapel it would be possible to make the change, but Esher pointed out that the space in the choir was small when the Chapel was full and it would be difficult and perhaps irreverent to attempt to turn the coffin round the other way. At last we came to the conclusion this would have to be done on the steps of the Mausoleum. We made the bearer parties try various methods, not carrying anything but merely walking slowly. When the relief took place the relieving party had to face the other way and slowly turn round before going into the Mausoleum. After one or two rehearsals this somewhat intricate manoeuvre worked perfectly. Eventually everything went smoothly and we dismissed the men.

If it had not been for Esher's forethought in having this rehearsal we should undoubtedly have had another fiasco.

Lord Edward Pelham-Clinton

Windsor Castle

Dull, and showery in afternoon. The Queen's funeral in St George's Chapel. The trains conveying the late Queen and all the Royalties arrive Windsor at 2 o'clock, after the procession through London – they, the King too, walk through the town with procession, enter at the Long-walk gate, through the quadrangle and so to St George's Chapel, The Royalties (70) lunch in dining-room.

Guests about 600 or 700 in St George's Hall.

A Royal dinner of 25. Household do-24.

Sunday, 3 February

Windsor

Sir Frederick Ponsonby

I was on the Castle Hill just before six and all the different people whom I had asked to help me arrived.

Remembering King Edward's remark that if anything went wrong he would never speak to me again, I had ordered ropes cut in suitable lengths and with hooks like traces to be kept hidden in a place in the Cloisters. The only person I told about this was Arthur Lloyd. In the unlikely event of the horses again kicking over the traces I gave him instructions that the Queen's Company was to pile arms and pull the gun-carriage as the sailors had done. I impressed on him the necessity of keeping this strictly confidential as the Artillery would undoubtedly be hurt if I had shown want of trust in them.

Bigge, who was most kind and forgiving, was invaluable, and discussed with the officers of the Artillery what should be done to ensure the horses being quiet. Ewart, with his great experience of processions and his knowledge of horses, joined these discussions, and I felt that as far as it was humanly possible to ensure that no mishap would occur again, every precaution was being taken.

We walked behind the gun-carriage along the whole route to the Mausoleum and I halted the procession at awkward places to see how the horses would behave, but everything went perfectly.

When the printer's proof of the ceremonial for Monday arrived, I took it to the King, who made several small alterations and sent it back to the printer. The rest of the day I spent in seeing the various officials and in arranging for tickets of admission into the private grounds of the Castle.

Randall Davidson, Bishop of Winchester

I did not go to early Service, remaining in bed till 10 o'clock. At 11 we had full Morning Prayer in St. George's, with Sermon by the Bishop of Oxford. He was not very audible, being really unwell. All the Royal Family were present, some in the Choir and some in the Royal Pew aloft.

Edmund H. Fellowes

About 2 minutes to 11 when we were all ready in the vestry the door suddenly opened and someone announced 'the King' and in walked the whole lot on their way up which is through the Vestry – about 15 of them and we saw them well. The King & Kaiser shook hands with the Dean and the Bishop of Winchester. The Queen & princesses had gone up earlier: most of the stalls were occupied by Royalties, the Duke of Connaught the Duchess of Albany & Princess Beatrice were in the stalls and just behind my stall were the 4 Battenberg children. I was rather nervous singing the service but fortunately it did not affect my voice: it was a queer sensation standing up to pronounce the absolution to such a congregation on their knees.

Randall Davidson, Bishop of Winchester

In the afternoon, at 3 p.m., I had to go with the King, Lord Esher, Lord Pembroke, and Fritz Ponsonby to the Mausoleum to arrange the details about Monday.

It had been most difficult to contrive the platform arrangements so as to enable the coffin to be properly lowered into the grave, but all was admirably done by Mr. Nutt.[16]

16 Alfred Young Nutt, clerk of works of Windsor Castle.

The Prince Consort's coffin was uncovered. It is of very much more reasonable dimensions than the needlessly huge coffin containing the shell with the little Queen. I think her coffin must be in external measurement at least one third larger than his, although of course he was a much larger person than she.

His was covered with velvet in accordance with the old custom; hers (unhappily by her own direction) was made to correspond with the great elm-wood coffins which disfigure the Royal Vault under the Albert Chapel.

It had been necessary to cut several inches from the inside of the granite sarcophagus to enable this great coffin of hers to be lowered, but all had been cleverly done. The King was very particular about the smallest details, and arranged where everyone should stand on the following day.

At 6 p.m. we had a Service in the Memorial Chapel, the Dean and I taking Prayers and Lesson, all of a special kind, and Madame Albani singing two solo Anthems. Her voice was too strong for the place, but the general effect of the Service in the darkness was very striking. All the Royal Family were present. Parratt played at a little harmonium placed near the Duke of Albany's Tomb.

Emma Albani

My mind looks for a moment to the most solemn and affecting incident of my whole career, when I was commanded to sing in the Memorial Chapel at Windsor over the coffin of Queen Victoria.

This took place about six o'clock in the afternoon. The chapel was very dimly lighted, and I sang '*Come unto Him*' and '*I know that my Redeemer liveth*' to the accompaniment of an harmonium played by Sir Walter Parratt, only the King, the Queen, and those members of the Royal Family who were then at Windsor being present. It was a terribly hard task, but the memory of the dear Queen and of all her goodness to me gave me courage, and I succeeded in this ordeal without breaking down. When I left, King

Edward was at the door with tears in his eyes. He thanked me and said '*Goodbye*'.

Lord Edward Pelham-Clinton

All the Royal Family attend Service in St George's Chapel at 11 – the suites in attendance go there also. The Bishop of Oxford preaches. I am not able to get out all day except to go to St George's. Ld Salisbury arrives at 6.15.

Royal dinner 27. Household do-35.

Monday, 4 February

Windsor

Sir Frederick Ponsonby

At 6 a.m. I again attended a short rehearsal with the horses. It was very cold and we kept them standing ten minutes before moving off, but they behaved perfectly.

After breakfast the King sent for me and I found him in the corridor. The list of Sovereigns and Princes staying in the Castle had been telegraphed to me by the clerk to the Master of the Household, but the name of the Duke of Fife[17] had been omitted. The curious part of this was that, although the King and several Court officials had seen the draft of the ceremonial, no one had noticed this omission. Unfortunately, the ceremonial had been published in the newspapers and everyone was reading it.

I found the German Emperor, the King of the Belgians,[18] and the King of Portugal[19] standing by the fire all smoking cigars,

17 Alexander Duff, 1st Duke of Fife (1849–1912). Married to Princess Louise, eldest daughter of King Edward VII.

18 Leopold II, King of the Belgians.

19 Carlos I, King of Portugal.

which rather shocked me as, of course, no one had ever smoked there before.

The King was standing a little further down the corridor with the Duke of Fife, and on seeing me proceeded to reprimand me severely. He said that the Duke of Fife's name had been omitted from the list and he could not understand how I could have made such a bad mistake. How could he have any confidence in me when I made omissions of this sort? It was inconceivable to him how anyone like me, accustomed to arrange ceremonies, should have omitted so important a person as his own son-in-law.

Naturally, I didn't say a word and the Duke of Fife, who seemed pleased to hear me abused, walked off satisfied. As soon as he had gone I said I could not apologise sufficiently for the mistake, which of course I ought to have seen and corrected when the proof came, but I reminded him that the proof had been on his table all Sunday and that no one else had noticed the omission. He at once became quite different and, taking me by the arm, said confidentially to me, '*I know how difficult it has been for you and I think you did wonders. I had to say something strong, as Fife was so hurt that he came to me and said he presumed that he could go to London as he was apparently not wanted.*'

Reginald Brett, Viscount Esher

To his son, Maurice

This morning I walked down to Frogmore with Lorne and was introduced to all the young Princes and Princesses. Played about with them for some time. Princess Beatrice of Coburg[20] is a beauty.

20 Princess Beatrice of Saxe-Coburg and Gotha (1884–1966). Granddaughter. Age 16. Daughter of Prince Alfred who had died the previous year.

Margaret of Connaught[21] a sweet. The Crown Prince is *charming*. Speaks English beautifully. But I fell in love with Albany.[22] He was quite unshy.

Duke of Argyll

On that last morning of this sad pilgrimage, one of those tales which, even if fanciful, possess a certain poetry, was heard to the effect that a child had noticed two gray doves fly out from St. George's archway to wing their way slowly in advance of the procession to the grounds to which the mourners were setting out. It revived in some the memory of the old belief that the dove, taking its place near the window of the dying, was the embodiment of another soul waiting to receive the one about to join it.

Reginald Brett, Viscount Esher

Of all the ceremonials, [this] was the simplest and most impressive. The procession from the Sovereign's entrance, the Princess of Wales leading Prince Edward of York,[23] the other children walking, was very touching and beautiful.

The Guardian

A Highlander walked sedately to and fro in the quadrangle, and a dozen naval officers, wearing straw hats and smart blue suits, marched up to the Queen's Porch and ranged themselves alongside.

21 Princess Margaret of Connaught (1882–1920). Granddaughter. Age 19. Eldest daughter of Arthur, Duke of Connaught.

22 Prince Charles, Duke of Saxe-Coburg and Gotha, Duke of Albany (1884–1954). Grandson. Age 16.

23 Prince Edward of York. Great-grandson. Age 6. Later King Edward VIII.

They were to bear the coffin from the mortuary chapel to the gun-carriage. It had been intended that this sad duty should fall to the Highlanders, but as they number only seven, the burden might have been too much for them. They were to act as bearers only in form.

Edmund H. Fellowes

We stood just outside the Sovereign's entrance. We saw them come out of the Quadrangle and walk the whole way down to the turn-off to Frogmore, which took them over 20 minutes as we saw them. It must have been extremely trying to them for all, particularly the Queen and princesses.

Everyone felt a little nervous about the horses drawing the gun carriage, they had to be patted and coaxed very much especially the two leaders.

Duke of Argyll

Again on a gun-carriage, this time horsed by bays, the artillery team proudly and quietly took their burden, and, followed by the family, the Queen was again taken through her ancient fortress.

This time it was down the descent towards the forest, and all those connected with Windsor were allowed to line the roadway, the Life Guards, in their long crimson cloaks, keeping clear the route. At the foot of the slope, the Guards relieved these, and the train of cloaked figures turned into the Frogmore road, which was kept private, save for the soldiers still forming a living avenue.

The pipers blew their lament in front, muffled drums rolled out plaintive notes of subdued sorrow, and the bands relieved them at intervals; and so, with lamentation and solemn dignity, her children and grandchildren and great-grandchildren following her, our dear Queen was brought to where she would be at rest beside her Prince.

Reginald Brett, Viscount Esher

At the Mausoleum, the arrangements were left to me. Everyone got into the Chapel, and the iron gates were closed, showing the soldiers without. Teddie and his guardsmen brought in the coffin. The King and the Princes and Princesses standing on the right. The choir on the left. The Bishop and Dean, and the two great Officers of State, at the head of the coffin. I stood close to the foot, but below the platform, in order to lift the rollers at the end of the service.

Randall Davidson, Bishop of Winchester

The arrangements were admirable, and the Service itself was touching beyond words. The music was beautifully sung, and, for the rest, we simply followed the Prayer Book Service, with the addition of a Prayer of thanksgiving for the Queen's life which I inserted before the Blessing.

Princess Marie-Louise

All the regal pomp and state fell away, and, to the pipes playing the Highland lament, '*Flowers of the Forest*', Victoria, Queen and Empress, attended by her family, was laid to rest by the side of the husband she had loved so dearly and for whom she had mourned so faithfully during those long, lonely years of her widowhood.

Duke of Argyll

In the tomb, sunk into the gray granite sarcophagus, his [Prince Albert] coffin was seen, and upon it lay the sword that he wore.

Her own was lifted, and then slowly lowered by her faithful Life Guards until it lay by his. For thirty-nine years the loving spirits had been separated. How long it seems, and yet what an unfelt moment in the being of the Eternal!

Randall Davidson, Bishop of Winchester

After the Blessing it had been arranged that the Royal Family should all pass in single file across the platform looking upon the grave in which the two coffins then lay side by side.

The King came first alone, but, instead of simply walking by, he knelt down by the grave. Then the Queen followed, leading the little Prince Edward by the hand. She knelt down, but the little boy was frightened, and the King took him gently and made him kneel beside him, and the three, in perfect silence, were there together – a sight not soon to be forgotten. Then they passed on and the Emperor came and knelt likewise, and so in turn all the rest of the Royal Family in a continuous string: Then the Household or at least the few who had been invited to be present.

As we left the building the rain or sleet began to fall. An hour later we drove to Bagshot to catch a train to Farnham, but before we reached Bagshot the snow was lying thickly on the ground, and everyone was commenting on the significant change of weather at the moment when it had ceased to matter.

So ended a fortnight as memorable certainly to me as any I am likely to see this side the grave.

Reginald Brett, Viscount Esher

To his son, Maurice

When they had gone, I remained to see the stone placed over the tomb and sealed.

Of all the mourners the Princess of Wales and the young Duke of Coburg displayed the most emotion. It was beautiful, interesting and pathetic. I brought away a laurel wreath that hung over the grave, which I shall have framed, and some lovely lilies of which I have kept some for you.

So ends the reign of the Queen – and now I feel for the first time that the new regime, so full of anxieties for England, has begun.

Sir Frederick Ponsonby

A curious incident happened at the last funeral ceremony.

An officer in khaki came to see me and applied for tickets for the Mausoleum. I told him that no one but the Royal Family would go to the Mausoleum, but I would give him a ticket for the private grounds. He was a dignified gentlemanly looking man with several medals.

I never gave him another thought, but it appeared that in some unaccountable way he stepped out of the crowd and joined the German suite in the procession. They very naturally thought he was connected with the arrangements and took no notice of him. However, I knew nothing of this.

When the gun-carriage reached the steps of the Mausoleum the two bearer parties did admirably. There was dead silence, no whispering or hesitation, simply the slow tread of the men. The doors were closed and the service began.

Suddenly a voice whispered in my ear, '*Who is the old bird with a beard?*' I looked round and saw the khaki officer, who was pointing to the King of the Belgians. I said '*Hush*', took him by the arm, led him to the door, and forcibly ejected him.

The service was really beautiful and the singing of the St. George's Chapel choir was perfect. At the conclusion of the service we all retired, leaving the Royal Family by the tomb.

When I got outside I espied my khaki friend and told him what I thought of his conduct. I said his behaviour was disgraceful and that I had not thought it possible that an officer of the Army should push himself forward and intrude in a purely family service like that. I added that I wanted his name and regiment as I should report him to the Commander-in-Chief. He gave me his name and regiment, saluted, and walked away.

We walked back to the Castle and on the way we were passed by carriages containing the Royal Family and their suites.

When I entered the Quadrangle I saw the Royal Family and foreign Sovereigns and Princes talking together at the Sovereign's Entrance, and in the midst of them was my khaki friend. He had apparently come up in a carriage with the German suite. I went off at once, took him by the arm, and much to the relief of the Royal Family, led him away to the gate, where I luckily found a policeman. I sent for one of the detectives and gave him instructions to take the officer to the station and send him off to London. I then wrote to the Military Secretary and reported the incident.

It later turned out that the poor man had been invalided home from South Africa suffering from sunstroke and that he was mentally deficient.

Lord Edward Pelham-Clinton

Dull and cold wind. Busy all the morning.

At 3 p.m. a procession leaves the Memorial Chapel for the final funeral of the Queen at Frogmore in the Mausoleum. A most beautiful and impressive ceremony altogether.

The King most kindly allows me to throw the earth on the coffin, during the well-known passage in the burial Service: the last, the very last ceremony that can be performed.

The Royal dinner is 23, Household dinner 30.

Sir James Reid

To his wife, Susan

The last act of the drama is over. All went well. No rain. The Procession was rather pathetic, all the Royalties (men and women) walking. The Service in the Mausoleum was most impressive. I send a few flowers from the 'grave', if it can be called so.

The King saw us all tonight and gave us the Victorian Order, Clinton, Edwards, Bigge, McNeill, and I got the 1st Class. So I am now G.C.V.O. (Promise!) The Kaiser has given me the star of my blue order [Star of Crown Order] which I had not got before, so now I have three stars! The King was very nice but said nothing about a pension! It will be so nice to be really with you and quite free.

Epilogue

Westminster Gazette

[The Queen outlived] all the members of the Privy Council who were alive in 1837; all the Peers who held their titles in 1837, except Earl Nelson, who was 14 in that year; and all the members who sat in the House of Commons on her accession to the throne.

She saw five Dukes of Norfolk succeed each other as Earl Marshal, and outlived every Duke and Duchess, and every Marquess and Marchioness who bore that rank in 1837.

Her Majesty saw eleven Lord Chancellors, ten Prime Ministers, six Speakers of the House of Commons, at least three bishops of every See, and five or six of many Sees, five Archbishops of Canterbury and six Archbishops of York, and six Commanders-in-Chief.

She saw eighteen presidents of the United States, eleven Viceroys of Canada, sixteen Viceroys of India, and France successively ruled by one King, one Emperor, and seven Presidents of a Republic.

One might note that Victoria also outlived all nine of her bridesmaids.

In a funeral at sea the ship is slowed down when the body is committed to the deep but once that has taken place there can be no waiting – the order is Full Steam Ahead. It is so with national affairs. Everything has been slowed down to do honour to our Queen, but the ship of state cannot tarry long.

Full steam ahead is today's order – just because it can be nothing else.

QUEEN'S INSTRUCTIONS IN CASE OF ILLNESS

Windsor Castle, 6 December 1875

The Queen wishes Sir William Jenner[1] to understand that it is her command that in case of serious illness she should only be attended by her own Doctors who always attend her, only calling in, after consultation with Princess Beatrice (supposing she was too ill to be herself consulted), any such Doctor or Surgeon whom her own professional Physicians knew the Queen liked, or thought fit to consult, or who was not a total stranger to herself, and not to yield to the pressure of any one of her other children, or any of her Ministers, for any one they might wish to name.

The Queen's daughters Princess Helena, Princess Louise and Princess Beatrice are fully aware of her wishes on the subject.

She wishes to add (which they likewise know) that she absolutely forbids anyone but her own four female attendants to nurse her and take care of her, as well as her faithful Personal Attendant, John Brown, whose strength, care, handiness, and gentleness make him invaluable at all times, and most peculiarly so in illness, and who was of such use and comfort to her during her long illness in 1871, in lifting and carrying and leading her, and who knows how to suggest anything for her comfort and convenience.

The Queen wishes no one therefore but J. Brown, whose faithfulness, tact and discretion are not to be exceeded, to help her female attendants in anything which may be required for her. In case he should require assistance, Lohlein,[2] her other personal attendant, and failing him any one person who Brown can entirely rely on, should give it.

1 Sir William Jenner, Physician in Ordinary to Queen Victoria – a position he retained until he retired and was replaced by Sir James Reid.

2 Rudolf Lohlein, former valet to Prince Albert.

Princess Beatrice, from living always with the Queen, is the one who is to be applied to for all that is to be done. If it is necessary to send for anyone of the rest of the family, it is on the express understanding that her wishes expressed in this memorandum should be strictly adhered to, and in no way departed from.

Her Physician should likewise inform the Prince and Princess of Wales, and any of her sons should they be there, of these her wishes, especially regarding the calling in of any additional medical man.

Her Privy Purse and Private Secretary should also be made aware of the Queen's orders on this point, so that they can resist the interference of any Minister.

The Queen wishes never to be deceived as to her real state.

This is to remain in force till such time as the Queen asks for this Memorandum.

Queen's Instructions for Burial

Instructions for my Dressers to be opened directly after my death and to be always taken about and kept by the one who may be travelling with me: when all are there the Senior always to keep it.

9 December, 1897

I wish to be buried in a white silk or cashmere dress, with a cap and white veil over my face with my wedding ring on and my diamond guard ring, given me by my beloved husband immediately after our marriage, and the plain gold ring with a single diamond in it, and the words 'Dieu La Garde' on it – the gift of my beloved Mother – my engagement ring with an emerald in the head of a golden snake, given to me by my dearly beloved Husband – Oct. 15 – 1839 – one similar to which (my gift) was buried with Him, – and an oxidised silver ring with my dear Husband's enamel, a small green enamelled ring, the first gift my dear Husband ever gave me – May 24 – 1836 – A gold ring with 3 Turquoises and 2 diamonds the gift of my dearest sister – a ring with five Scotch pearls, the gift of my dear daughter Louise, a small gold one with three pearls and small diamonds, the gift of my darling child Beatrice – all continually worn by me – as well as a plain gold wedding ring which had belonged to the Mother of My dear valued servant J. Brown, and was given him by her in 75 – which he wore for a short time and I have worn constantly since his death – to be on my fingers.

I wish the small chain which I always wear round my neck – and to which are attached a diamond Locket containing my beloved Husband's hair, which was given me in 1839 by my Aunt, the late Queen Louise of the Belgians, which I have worn ever since, and seven small Lockets, 2 of which with painted Photographs of my beloved Husband and dearest Mother, and the others containing the hair of near and dear ones, would be placed on the same chain which is to be worn round my neck – as well as any other small Lockets which might hereafter be added – I wish a small granite one set in gold containing a piece of Balmoral heather and the hair of a friend, which is attached to my watch chain, to be added to this chain – also a small quartz heart – 3 golden lockets, one of these containing the hair of our valued friend Baron Stockmar who died in 1863 – Another with a diamond in the centre containing the hair of my dear friend the late Countess Blucker, and one in gold and a pearl in the centre, containing the hair of my dear friend the late Lady Augusta Stanley to be attached to a small golden chain to be worn on my right arm – A round blue Enamel Locket containing the hair of my 9 children which I always wear when I am in mourning, as well as a bracelet of plain gold with a single Turquoise on it, which had belonged to my dearest Mother, to be on my left arm.

One of the Brooches, the gift of my dearest Husband, to be selected by Beatrice to be fastened to my dress – I wish the painted profile Photograph of my dearest Husband, always on my dressing table and a coloured Photograph or miniature of my dearest Beatrice and one of her dear Husband, the photographs of all my dear children and their Husband and wives and of my grandchildren in frames.

A coloured profile Photograph in a leather case of my faithful friend J. Brown, his gift to me – with some of his hair laid with it and some of the photographs – which I have marked with a X – and have often carried in a silk case, (worked by my faithful Annie McDonald) in my pocket, to be put in the case, in my hand, and the cast of my beloved Husband's hand which is always near me to be placed in my coffin near me.

All these objects which have been so dear to me during my life time and have never left me – I should wish to be near my earthly remains.

In addition to all these, I should wish the pocket Handkerchief of my dearest Husband and one of his cloaks, a shawl worked by my dearest daughter Alice, and a pocket handkerchief of my faithful Brown, that friend who was more devoted to me than anyone, to be laid on me. Some souvenir of my faithful wardrobe maid Annie McDonald to be near me, and anything else which Beatrice should wish to add.

(Signed)
Victoria RI

The British Medical Journal

The Last Illness of the Queen.

The Queen's health for the past 12 months had been failing, with symptoms mainly of a dyspeptic kind accompanied by impaired general nutrition, periods of insomnia, and later by occasional slight and transitory attacks of aphasia, the latter suggesting that the cerebral vessels had become damaged, although Her Majesty's general arterial system showed remarkably few signs of age.

The constant brain work through a long life of Royal responsibilities, and the Imperial events, domestic sorrows, and anxieties which have crowded into her later years, may no doubt be held in some measure to account for this discrepancy between the cerebral and general vessel nutrition. The thoracic and abdominal organs showed no signs of disease.

The dyspepsia which tended to lower Her Majesty's originally robust constitution was especially marked during her last visit to Balmoral. It was there that the Queen first manifested distinct symptoms of brain fatigue and lost notably in weight.

These symptoms continued at Windsor where in November and December slight aphasic symptoms were first observed, always of an ephemeral kind and unattended by any motor paralysis.

Although it was judged best to continue the negotiations for Her Majesty's proposed visit to the continent in the spring, it was distinctly recognised by her physicians and by those in closest personal attendance upon her that these arrangements were purely provisional, it being particularly desired not to discourage Her Majesty in regard to her own health by suggesting doubts as to the feasibility of the change abroad to which she had been looking forward.

The Queen suffered unusual fatigue from the journey to Osborne on Dec.18th, showing symptoms of nervous agitation and restlessness which lasted for two days. Her Majesty afterwards improved for a time both in appetite and nerve tone in response to more complete quietude than she had hitherto consented to observe.

A few days before the final illness transient but recurrent symptoms of apathy and somnolence with aphasic indications and increasing feebleness gave great uneasiness to her physician.

On Wednesday, January 16th, the Queen showed increasing symptoms of cerebral exhaustion. By an effort of will, however, Her Majesty would for a time, as it were, command her brain to work and the visitor of a few minutes would fail to observe the signs of cerebral exhaustion.

On Thursday the exhaustion was more marked with considerable drowsiness; and a slight flattening was observed on the right side of the face. From this time the aphasia and facial paresis although incomplete were permanent.

On Friday the Queen was a little brighter, but on Saturday evening, 19th, there was a relapse of the graver symptoms which with remissions continued until the end.

It is important to note that notwithstanding the great bodily weakness and cerebral exhaustion the heart's action was steadily maintained to the last; the pulse at times evincing increased tension, but being always regular and of normal frequency.

The temperature was normal throughout. In the last few hours of life paresis of the pulmonary nerves set in, the heart beating steadily to the end.

Beyond the slight right facial flattening there was never any motor paralysis, and except for the occasional lapses mentioned the mind cannot be said to have been clouded. Within a few minutes of death the Queen recognised the several members of her family.

THE MAROCHETTI FIGURE

Reginald Brett, Viscount Esher

Last year the Queen mentioned to me that there was a recumbent figure of herself in existence at Windsor. Last week, I asked the Clerk of the Works where it was kept. He had never heard of it. No one had heard of it, and there was much scepticism. After a minute enquiry, an old workman remembered that about 1865 the figure had been walled up in the stores at Windsor. The brickwork was taken down, and the figure found. It was pure chance that it was discovered.

It is now over the tomb, a really impressive thing by Marochetti. To-day I walked down to the Mausoleum, still embowered in flowers, to see the recumbent figure. It is a graceful effigy. The Queen as she was in 1861.

Members Stand

House of Commons
Mr. Lough (Islington, W.): I beg to ask the First Lord of the Treasury who was responsible for placing the stand allotted to Members of the Houses of Parliament at the funeral of Her late Majesty at so great a distance from the route of the procession.

Mr. Akers Douglas, First Commissioner of Works, (St Augustine's): The route of the funeral of her late Majesty was selected and the general arrangements, made by the Earl Marshal, and were not under the control of the Government. It is a matter of regret to me that no better provision could be made.

Mr. Alfred Davies (Carmarthen Boroughs): May I ask how it was there were no covers on this stand?

Mr. Akers Douglas: There was literally no time to put up a cover, and I doubt whether we should have been justified in putting it up, thereby excluding the view of those behind.

Mr. Alfred Davies: May I also ask if it would not have been better to have had no place at all than such a stand?

Sir E. Ashmead-Bartlett (Sheffield Ecclesall): Were any steps taken by the right hon. Gentleman or any other person in responsible authority to represent to the Earl Marshal that the position of the stand or the route of the procession was most inconvenient for Members of the House?

Mr. Akers Douglas: I have said that there was very short time. This was literally the only accommodation that could be found.

THE CATHOLIC ARGUMENT

Baron Eckardstein

King Edward expressed himself very strongly as to the attitude of the English Roman Catholic clergy, who had refused to hold memorial services on the day of the Queen's funeral because she had not belonged to the one true Church.

Marie Corelli [3]

The unnecessary announcement made by Leo XIII to the effect that he was 'unwilling to be represented at the funeral of a Protestant Queen' and also the equally gratuitous information given out in all the Roman Catholic Churches that 'no Masses would be offered up for the soul of the Queen'. The Imperial English nation has not asked for 'Masses' for its late Queen, nor did His Majesty the King and Emperor supplicate the Pope to represent himself at the world famed Obsequies.

Letters to The Times*:*

Sir, – It ought to be known that keen regret, not unmixed with indignation, is felt by large numbers of English Catholics at the action of our ecclesiastical authorities in separating us from the rest of our fellow-countrymen at this moment of national mourning.

Yours obediently,
Robert Edward Dell[4]

3 Best-selling author of romantic novels and a favourite of Queen Victoria, who had a collection of all her books.

4 Robert Dell, a Catholic modernist, received into the Church in 1897.

Sir, – May I be permitted to express my utter astonishment that either Catholics or non-Catholics should expect, or even desire, masses to be offered up for our late beloved Queen, considering that on her accession to the Throne she publicly declared, among other things, 'The sacrifice of the mass as now used in the Church of Rome to be superstitious and idolatrous'?

However great our love and reverence for her memory may be – and we yield to none in our loyalty – it should hardly lead us to perform on her behalf a sacred rite which she herself so solemnly and so unsparingly condemned.

That non-Catholics should declare the mass to be superstitious and idolatrous in one breath, and that, in the next, they should complain that such 'a superstitious and idolatrous' rite was not offered up for the Queen, will strike the impartial observer as less than reasonable.

Yours,

Monsignor John Vaughan[5]

Sir, – Monsignor John Vaughan, in his letter of yesterday to The Times, misses the point. That the Mass should be reviled in the Protestant official coronation oath is surely no reason why a Catholic should depart from the Christian rule of praying for those who err, or who have erred, in ignorance. And the worthiest form of prayer that Catholics can offer for the living and for the dead is the Holy Mass.

Frederick Rolfe[6]

Sir, – Mgr. John Vaughan's argument is ingenious rather than ingenuous. If it has any validity it is valid no less against private than against public Masses. Yet Mgr. Vaughan must know that there

---

5 John Vaughan, came from a deeply religious Roman Catholic family; five of his sisters became nuns and six of his brothers took Holy Orders. He became a Roman Catholic bishop and his eldest brother became Archbishop of Westminster.

6 Frederick Rolfe, also known as Baron Corvo, he was dismissed from the priesthood on two occasions and in later life wrote his most famous novel, *Hadrian the Seventh*.

is nothing to prevent a priest from saying a private Mass for the repose of the soul of her late Majesty or from offering the ordinary Mass of the day for that intention. As a fact such Masses are said for deceased Protestants every day and many have been said for Queen Victoria; it is reported, indeed, that the Pope himself said one.

If the public Mass of Requiem for non-Catholics is still forbidden it is probably for the reason stated by Cardinal Manning when he wrote in 1887 of the Roman congregation, 'Their pride will not let them say after all that the earth moves.'

Yours obediently,
Robert Edward Dell

Sir, – It is natural that a brother should stand up for a brother; but, this conceded, the letter of Mgr. John Vaughan is a poor cloak to cover up the serious blunder made by the Cardinal. In the eyes of many educated – if not all – Roman Catholics, the Cardinal's pastoral to his flock is (1) illogical, (2) doctrinally unsound, (3) uncharitable, and (4) impolite. I write in the name of several priests.

Alas! our present Cardinal is no statesman, and never knows when to speak the proper word; every public action and pastoral of his has been a blunder; we pity him and we grieve for our position under his leadership.

One of his Westminster Priests.

Sir, – Your Catholic correspondents who seek to defend the conduct of Cardinal Vaughan do not understand the attitude of others on this matter. It is not that we attribute any efficacy in Requiem Masses or think them superstitious. We are touched at hearing that African chiefs have ordered tom-toms to be beaten or cattle sacrificed for the repose of the soul of the Great White Queen. What pleases the subjects of the Queen is the expression of devotion by men of all races and religions. The Catholic Church, through Cardinal Vaughan, has struck a discordant note.

I am, Sir, your obedient servant,
Spectator

Funeral Expenses

House of Commons

Mr. Keir Hardie (Merthyr Tydfil): referred to the Printing and Stationery Vote, a portion of which was required for mourning stationery in connection with the death of the late Queen. He thought the Government might have set a better standard of taste in regard to the stationery. Its hideous black border was offensive to the eye and the taste.

He had no objection whatever to the amount spent on the funeral ceremony [£35,500]; his objection was entirely to the manner in which the money had been expended.

The ceremony took the form of a military funeral, and he protested in the strongest and most emphatic manner against the Head of a constitutional State being buried with military honours, to the total exclusion of the whole civil and religious life of the community.

A part of the Vote was for stands erected along the route of the procession. He recalled with a feeling of shame that he had the honour of occupying a position on one of those stands. There were three stands erected, one for the veterans of the Army, one for cadets being trained for the Army, and the third for Members of the House of Commons.

The dignified part which the representatives of the people of England were called upon to play in the funeral ceremonies of England's greatest Queen was to stand on tip-toe upon a stand some thirty yards away from the procession in order to obtain a glimpse of it as it passed along. Whoever was responsible for the making of those arrangements was guilty of an insult to the nation at large and to the House of Commons in particular.

What he felt then, and what he felt now was that the dead body of England's Queen was used as a recruiting sergeant to help the military designs now being carried into effect.

If anything were required to mark the decadence of England's greatness they had it in the fact that the House of Commons, composed of English gentlemen, was prepared to see its high position taken from it, and the soldier placed where the ruler by right should stand.

Who was responsible for the arrangements in connection with the funeral of the late Queen, and why it was that the funeral was turned into a military display from which the civil life of the nation was altogether eliminated?

Sir M. Hicks Beach, The Chancellor of the Exchequer (Bristol. W.): I now come to the point to which the hon. Member called attention, the expenses of the funeral of her late Majesty the Queen.

The hon. Member has not expressed, and I am quite sure that no one would express, any objection to the amount of the Vote, but he has called attention to the manner in which the funeral appeared to him to have been conducted.

He has described it as a military pageant from which the civil and religious elements were entirely absent, and he has stated that in his opinion that solemn procession through 'the streets of the metropolis was viewed merely as a pageant by the hundreds and thousands of spectators, and not with feelings of reverence.' I do not think that would be the impression of anyone else who witnessed it.

If there was a military element in the funeral it was largely necessitated by the fact that it was impossible to keep the streets without the presence of the military, and no one, so far as I am aware, has expressed any objection to this except the hon. Member himself.

I am persuaded that though there was a certain amount of military ceremony in the funeral, it was not more than was right and proper in the funeral of a Sovereign of this country, that the ceremony was solemn, quiet, and reverent, and that certainly both the civil and religious elements were adequately represented.

The hon. Member has found fault with the accommodation reserved for the House of Commons. I have nothing to do with arrangements of that kind. All the arrangements for the funeral were under the supreme control of the Duke of Norfolk, the Earl Marshal, who, I think, the House will remember was not long ago responsible for similar arrangements on the occasion of the public funeral of Mr. Gladstone, and who, I believe, conducted on both occasions the arrangements entrusted to him in a manner deserving praise. I do not think the hon. Member is justified in the remarks he has made, and I think it was perfectly evident that they did not meet with the sympathy of the House.

QUEEN VICTORIA'S SILK PALL

Sir Lionel Cust[7]

At the time of Queen Victoria's funeral, a rich silk Pall had been worked by the Royal School of Needlework, and had covered the coffin during the whole proceedings, until the Queen's body had been placed finally in the Royal Mausoleum at Frog-more. The Pall had then been taken off, together with the National Flag and the Gilt Crown and Cushion, which had also been laid upon the coffin, and entrusted to the care of Mr. Miles until further orders.

No instructions had ever been received by Mr. Miles since the Queen's Funeral, and he now asked me if I could help him to some course of action. I at once took an opportunity of informing King Edward, who thanked me most warmly for this reminder, and commanded me to have the Pall and other objects packed up ready for me to bring to Osborne myself, whenever the King should be able to pay another visit.

This opportunity came when the King was going down to make a formal inspection of the new Hospital for Officers.[8] I received

7 Sir Lionel Cust was appointed a Gentleman Usher and Surveyor of Pictures in Ordinary to His Majesty in 1901.

8 Osborne House had been gifted to the nation by King Edward VII and in 1904 it opened as the King Edward VII Convalescent Home for Officers.

a command to join a party of various officials at Portsmouth, and to bring the Pall and other objects with me to Osborne.

The next morning we went by special steamer to Cowes, and so up to Osborne, where we met the King and his party. On arrival at Osborne I delivered up my parcel, in accordance with commands, to Miss Haines, the matron of the Hospital, and then waited on events, not knowing what was going to happen.

The King was taken over the new Hospital in the great wing of the house, conducted by Sir Frederick Treves,[9] Sir Schomberg McDonnell, Lord Esher, and others connected with the administration of the Hospital, but when he came to the iron grille, which separated this wing from the central part of the house, the 'Pavilion,' which was to be kept private, the King stopped the party, and beckoning to Prince Louis of Battenberg and myself, conducted us across the passage into the late Queen's apartments.

There, in the room in which Queen Victoria died, we found Miss Haines waiting for us. King Edward, who had evidently thought out exactly what to do, then signed to us to come forward, and each take one corner of the Pall, which we then laid reverently upon the death-bed of the great Queen, the King, Prince Louis, Miss Haines and myself each holding one corner, until all was in order. We then laid on the Pall the National Flag and the Crown and Cushion. In front of the bed a small altar was placed with suitable accessories. This was all carried out with great solemnity, almost in silence, and the King was evidently struggling against deep emotion. When it was all over the King returned to rejoin the Hospital party.

It would not be easy to forget a scene of such poignant intimacy as that which took place in the death chamber of Queen Victoria on this occasion.

---

9 Sir Frederick Treves. Sergeant-surgeon to the King. He had operated on the King just before his coronation to drain an abscess. He also wrote a book about his patient, Joseph Merrick, known as the Elephant Man.

The Family of Queen Victoria in January 1901

9 Children (3 deceased)
39 Grandchildren (9 deceased)
42 Great-grandchildren (1 deceased)

Queen Victoria (1819–1901) m. †Prince Albert of Saxe-Coburg and Gotha (1819–61)

Victoria, Empress Frederick of Germany, *Vicky* (1840–1901)

Albert Edward, Prince of Wales, *Bertie* (1841–1910)

†Alice, Grand Duchess of Hesse and by Rhine (1843–78)

†Alfred, Duke of Saxe-Coburg and Gotha (1844–1900)

Helena, Princess Christian of Schleswig-Holstein, *Lenchen* (1846–1923)

Louise, Duchess of Argyll (1848–1939)

Arthur, Duke of Connaught and Strathearn (1850–1942)

†Leopold, Duke of Albany (1853–84)

Beatrice, Princess Henry of Battenberg (1857–1944)

Victoria, Empress Frederick of Germany (1840–1901) m. †Prince Frederick of Prussia later Emperor Frederick III of Germany (1831–88)

Wilhelm II, Emperor of Germany (1859–1941) m. Princess Augusta of Schleswig-Holstein-Sonderburg-Augustenberg (1858–1921)

Wilhelm, the German Crown Prince, Crown Prince of Prussia (1882–1951)
Prince Eitel (1883–1942)
Prince Adalbert (1884–1948)
Prince August (1887–1949)
Prince Oskar (1888–1958)
Prince Joachim (1890–1920)
Princess Viktoria (1892–1980)

Charlotte (1860–1919) m. Prince Bernard of Saxe-Meiningen (1851–1928)

Princess Feodora of Saxe-Meiningen (1879–1945)

Prince Henry of Prussia (1862–1929) m. Princess Irene of Hesse and by Rhine (1866–1953)

Prince Waldemar (1899–1945)
Prince Sigismund (1896–1978)
Prince Heinrich (1900–04)

†Sigismund, Prince Sigismund of Prussia (1864–66)

Viktoria (1866–1929) m. Prince Adolf of Schaumburg-Lippe (1859–1916)

†Waldemar, Prince Waldemar of Prussia (1868–79)

Sophia (1870–1932) m. Constantine, Crown Prince of Greece (1868–1923)

Prince George (1890–1947)
Prince Alexander (1893–1920)
Princess Helen (1896–1982)

Margaret (1872–1954) m. Prince Frederick Charles of Hesse (1868–1940)

Prince Friedrich (1893–1916)
Prince Maximilian (1894–1914)
Prince Philipp (1896–1980)
Prince Wolfgang (1896–1989)

Albert Edward, Prince of Wales (1841–1910) m. Princess Alexandra of Denmark, *Alix* (1844–1925)

†Albert Victor, Duke of Clarence & Avondale, *Eddy* (1864–92)

George, Duke of York (1865–1936) m. Princess Victoria Mary of Teck, *May* (1867–1953)

Prince Edward (1894–1972) later King Edward VIII
Prince Albert (1895–1952) later King George VI
Princess Mary (1897–1965) later Countess of Harewood
Prince Henry (1900–74) later Duke of Gloucester

Louise (1867–1931) m. Alexander Duff, 1st Duke of Fife (1849–1912)

†Alastair Duff, Marquess of Fife (1890)
Lady Alexandra Duff (1891–1959)
Lady Maud Duff (1893–1945)

Victoria, Princess Victoria of Wales, *Toria* (1868–1935)

Maud (1869–1938) m. Prince Carl of Denmark (1872–1957)

†Alexander, Prince Alexander John of Wales (1871)

†Alice, Grand Duchess of Hesse and by Rhine (1843–78) m. †Louis, Grand Duke of Hesse and by Rhine (1837–92)

Victoria (1863–1950) m. Prince Louis of Battenberg (1854–1921)

Princess Alice (1885–1969) mother of Prince Philip, Duke of Edinburgh
Princess Louise (1889–1965)
Prince George (1892–1938)
Prince Louis (1900–79) later Lord Mountbatten of Burma

Elisabeth, *Ella* (1864–1918) m. Grand Duke Sergei Alexandrovich of Russia (1857–1905)

Irene (1866–1953) m. Prince Henry of Prussia (1862–1929)

Prince Waldemar (1889–1945)
Prince Sigismund (1896–1978)
Prince Heinrich (1900–04)

Ernest Louis, Grand Duke of Hesse and by Rhine (1868–1937) m. Princess Victoria Melita of Saxe-Coburg and Gotha, *Ducky* (1876–1936) div. 1901

Princess Elisabeth (1895–1903)

†Friedrich, Prince Friedrich of Hesse and by Rhine (1870–73)

Alix (1872–1918) m. Tsar Nicholas II (1868–1918)

Grand Duchess Olga (1895–1918)

Grand Duchess Tatiana (1897–1918)

Grand Duchess Maria (1899–1918)

†Marie, Princess Marie of Hesse and by Rhine (1874–78)

†Alfred, Duke of Saxe-Coburg and Gotha (1844–1900) m. Grand Duchess Maria Alexandrovna of Russia (1853–1920)

---

†Alfred, The Hereditary Prince of Saxe-Coburg and Gotha, Duke of Saxony, *Young Affie* (1874–99)

Marie, *Missy* (1875–1938) m. Ferdinand, Crown Prince of Romania (1865–1927)

Prince Carol (1893–1953)

Princess Elisabeth (1894–1956)

Princess Maria (1900–61)

Victoria Melita, *Ducky* (1876–1936) m. Ernest Louis, Grand Duke of Hesse and by Rhine (1868–1937) div. 1901

Princess Elisabeth (1895–1903)

Alexandra, *Sandra* (1878–1942) m. Prince Ernst of Hohenlohe-Langenburg (1863–1950)

Prince Gottfried (1897–1960)

Princess Marie Melita (1899–1967)

Beatrice, Princess Beatrice of Saxe-Coburg and Gotha, *Baby Bee* (1884–1966)

Helena, Princess Christian of Schleswig-Holstein, *Lenchen* (1846–1923) m. Prince Christian of Schleswig-Holstein (1831–1917)

---

†Christian, Prince Christian Victor of Schleswig-Holstein, *Christle* (1867–1900)

Albert, Prince Albert of Schleswig-Holstein, *Abby* (1869–1931)

Helena, Princess Helena Victoria of Schleswig-Holstein, *Thora* (1870–1948)

Marie Louise, Princess Marie-Louise of Schleswig-Holstein, *Louie* (1872–1956) m. Prince Aribert of Anhalt (1866–1933) annul. 1900

†Prince Harald of Schleswig-Holstein (1876)

Louise, Duchess of Argyll (1848–1939) m. John Campbell, Marquess of Lorne, later 9th Duke of Argyll (1845–1914)

Arthur, Duke of Connaught and Strathearn (1850–1942) m. Princess Luise Margarete of Prussia, *Louischen* (1860–1917)

Margaret, Princess Margaret of Connaught, *Daisy* (1882–1920)

Arthur, Prince Arthur of Connaught (1883–1938)

Patricia, Princess Patricia of Connaught, *Patsy* (1886–1974)

†Leopold, Duke of Albany (1853–84) m. Princess Helena of Waldeck-Pyrmont (1861–1922)

Alice, Princess Alice of Albany (1883–1981)

Charles Edward, Duke of Saxe-Coburg and Gotha (1884–1954)

Beatrice, Princess Henry of Battenberg, *Baby* (1857–1944) m. †Henry, Prince of Battenberg, *Liko* (1858–96)

Alexander, Prince Alexander of Battenberg (1886–1960)

Victoria, Princess Victoria Eugenie of Battenberg, *Ena* (1887–1969)

Leopold, Prince Leopold of Battenberg, *Young Leopold* (1889–1922)

Maurice, Prince Maurice of Battenberg (1891–1914)

Sources & Permissions

Albani, Emma, *Forty Years of Song* (Mills & Boon, 1911)
Arthur, Max, *Lost Voices of the Edwardians* (by permission of HarperCollins Publishers Ltd © Max Arthur, 2006)
Asquith, Margot, *Autobiography of Margot Asquith* (Penguin, 1936)
Barlow, Sir Thomas, *Letter to his Brother* (by permission of Dr Claire Y. Barlow, Wellcome Collection (PP/BAR/B/2/4))
Battersea, Constance Flower, Baroness, *Reminiscences* (Macmillan & Co., 1922)
Bennett, Arnold, *Journals of Arnold Bennett*, ed. Newman Fowler (Cassell & Co., 1932)
Blunt, Wilfrid Scawen, *My Diaries 1888–1914* (Martin Secker, 1932)
Brett, Reginald, Viscount Esher, *Journals & Letters of Reginald Brett, Viscount Esher*, ed. Maurice V. Brett (Ivor Nicholson & Watson, 1934)
Cambridge, George, Duke of Cambridge, *A Memoir, Vol. II 1871–1904*, ed. Edgar Sheppard (Longmans, Green & Co., 1906)
Campbell, John, 9th Duke of Argyll, *The Life of Queen Victoria* (George Bell & Sons, 1909)
Cecil, Violet, *My Picture Gallery, 1886–1901, Viscountess Milner* (John Murray Press, 1951, an imprint of Hodder & Stoughton, by permission of the Lord Hardinge of Penshurst)
Corelli, Marie, *The Passing of a Great Queen* (Dodd Mead & Co., 1901)
Cust, Sir Lionel, *King Edward VII and his Court: Some Reminiscences* (John Murray, 1930)
Daily Chronicle, 1901
Daily Express, 1901
Daily News, 1901
Daily Telegraph, 1901
Davidson, Randall (courtesy of Lambeth Palace Library (RD Vol XIX: 101))
Duff, David, *The Shy Princess: The Life of Her Royal Highness Princess Beatrice* (Allen & Unwin, 1959)
Eckardstein, Baron von, *Ten Years at the Court of St James' 1895–1905*, trans. & ed. George Young (Thornton Butterworth, 1921)
Fellowes, Rev. E.H., Fellowes Papers (Oriel College Archives)
Fergusson, Gordon, *James Cecil: Hounds are Home: The History of the*

Royal Calpe Hunt (by permission of Mr J.C.T. Dalton. Springwood Books, 1979)

Fitzroy, Sir Almeric W., *Memoirs, Vol. 1* (G.H. Doran, 1925)

Frye, Kate (courtesy of Elizabeth Crawford, www.womanandsphere.com, Royal Holloway Archives)

Gleichen, Lady Helena, *Contacts and Contrasts* (John Murray, 1940)

Gower, Lord Ronald Charles Sutherland, *Old Diaries 1881–1901* (John Murray, 1902)

Haggard, Sir H. Rider, *The Days of my Life, Vol. 2*, ed. C.J. Longman (Longmans Green & Co., 1926)

Hamilton, Sir Edward, Hamilton Papers (courtesy of British Library (Vol. LXXXVI ff. 1+139, 27 Aug 1900–8 Mar 1901, Add MS 48677))

Holland, Caroline, *Notebooks of a Spinster Lady 1878–1903* (Cassell, 1919)

Lang, Cosmo (courtesy of Lambeth Palace Library (Lang, Vol. 223))

Lee, Sir Sidney, *King Edward VII: A Biography* (Macmillan & Co., 1927)

London Gazette, 1901

Lubbuck, Percy, *The Letters of Henry James* (Macmillan and Co., 1920)

Lytton, Lady Edith (courtesy of Knebworth House, www.knebworthhouse.com)

Mallet, Marie, Mallet Family Papers (courtesy of the Master and Fellows, Balliol College, by permission of Professor John Mallet)

Marie-Louise, Princess, *My Memories of Six Reigns* (Evans Brothers, 1956)

Markham, Violet R., *Return Passage: The Autobiography of Violet R. Markham* (by permission of Oxford University Press)

McDonnell, Louisa, *Recollections of Louisa, Countess of Antrim* (The Kings Stone Press, 1937)

Merrill, Arthur Lawrence, *Life & Times of Queen Victoria* (National Publishing Co., 1901)

Monkswell, Lady Mary, *A Victorian Diarist: Extracts from the Journals of Mary, Lady Monkswell*, ed. E.C.F. Collier (John Murray, 1946)

New York Times, 1901

Packard, Jerrold M., *Farewell in Splendour* (Dutton, 1995)

Pelham-Clinton, Lord, *Leaves from my Diary, 1901 Jan–Feb, Guide to the Lord Pelham-Clinton Papers, 1838–1907* (David M. Rubenstein Rare Book & Manuscript Library, Duke University)

Ponsonby, Sir Frederick, *Recollections of Three Reigns* (Eyre and Spotiswoode, 1951)

Ramm, Agatha, *Beloved & Darling Child* (Alan Sutton, 1990)

Reid, Sir James, *Ask Sir James* (Hodder & Stoughton, 1987, by permission of Lady Michaela Reid)

Rennell, Tony, *Last Days of Glory* (Viking, 2000)

Royal Archives: by permission of Her Majesty Queen Elizabeth II: RA VIC/MAIN/QVJ/1900, RA VIC/MAIN/QVJ/1901, RA VIC/

ADDA17/970, RA VIC/ADDA17/971, RA VIC/MAIN/F/23/9, RA VIC/MAIN/F/23/9a, RA VIC/MAIN/F/23/14, RA VIC/MAIN/F/23/39, RA QM/PRIV/CC/22/56; RA QM/PRIV/CC/22/57; QM/PRIV/CC/29/4

The Standard, 1901

The Times, 1901

Westminster Gazette, 1901

Wilhelm II, *My Memoirs*, trans. Thomas R. Ybarra (Cassell, 1922)

Wodehouse, John, *The Journal of John Wodehouse First Earl of Kimberley, 1862–1902*, eds Angus Hawkins and John Powell © Royal Historical Society, 1997, published by Cambridge University Press

ACKNOWLEDGEMENTS

Thank you to Ruth Dooley for introducing me to Sir James Reid, and thank you to Tony Morris for introducing me to Laura Perehinec and The History Press. Thank you to Julie Crocker at the Royal Archives and thank you to the Lambeth Palace Library, the Balliol Archive and the Oriel Archive. And thank you to Dr. Catherine Henstridge for introducing me to the Bodleian and the mysteries of the Gladstone link.

Index of Names